The 6 Step Approach to Embracing

Project Management

For Increased Personal, Professional, and Business Success

Really Simplified

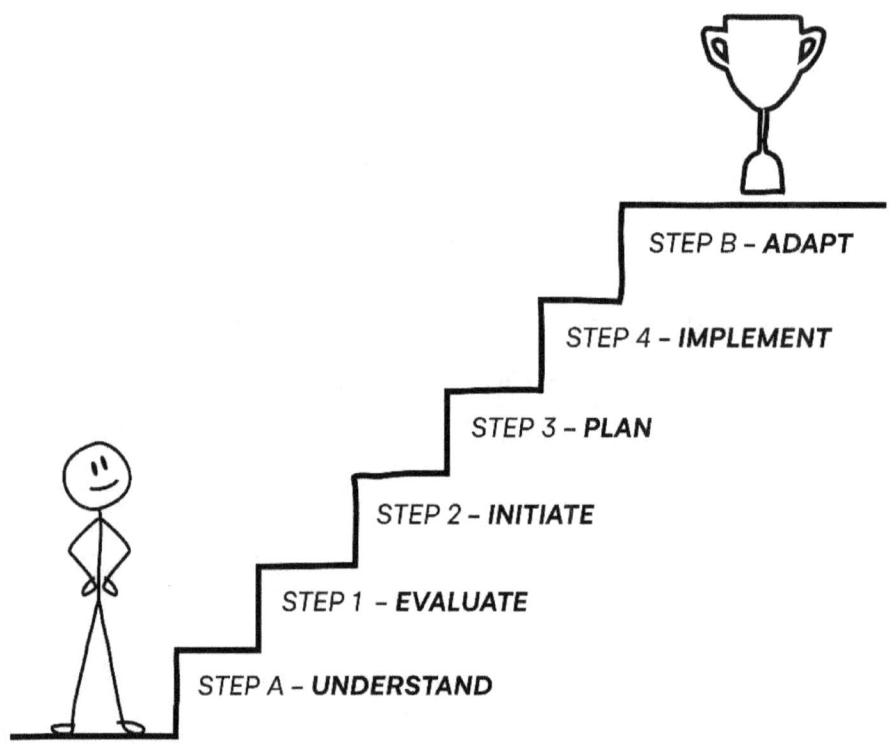

Copyright © 2021

David Gadish – All Rights Reserved

This book may not be reproduced without the written permission of the author and publisher.

Printed in the United States of America

ISBN: 978-1-954713-06-2

BH4 Publishing

This book is dedicated to the thousands of students that have had to tolerate my stories over the years at California State University, Los Angeles. You have taught me so much!

    And of course, I always enjoy the occasional "Hey Gadish, how are you?" when I go shopping at the home depot.

Motivation

Over the past three decades, I have had the privilege to interact with thousands of people through my decade-long corporate career, followed by two decades of operating my businesses, coaching, mentoring, and teaching.

I have spent almost two decades as a professor at California State University, Los Angeles, teaching project management using various books, primarily based on the Project Management Institute's methodology for managing projects. I always thought that the methodology, as presented, was not straightforward to understand and implement.

*****

Additionally, all around me, I see good people that spend many hours each week watching TV, engaged in various social media platforms, with little time left to make progress with their own lives. And when they do get to taking care of their own future, I find that many lack the tools to do so in a way that maximizes the benefit for them in the little time that they are willing to commit to themselves.

*****

I wonder how many people, in this fast-changing world, lose some of the control they believe they had over their lives, end up depressed. I wonder, how many end up jealous of others. I do know that jealousy can lead to hate.

*****

I hope that this book and my perspective will allow you to gain more control over your life and increase your personal, professional and business success!

Overview

The book presents a 6-step approach to **embracing** project management for increased personal, professional, and business success. The Understand, Evaluate, Initiate, Plan, Implement and Adapt (UEI-PIA) approach reflects the author's experiences which include managing countless projects:

- For private sector and government organization during his decade in the corporate world
- For his government, for-profit, non-profit clients during his management consulting years
- For his own businesses and personal life

It also reflects his nearly 20 years of teaching project management at California State University, Los Angeles.

The UEI-PIA Approach Introduced

The UEI-PIA Approach, developed by the author and based on the Project Management Institute's project management methodology, and consists of the following six steps:

Understand (Step A) – You will learn to better understand yourself, your goals, and the opportunities in your life. You will understand the benefits of bringing project management methodology into your professional, business, and personal life.

Evaluate (Step 1) – You will learn to evaluate the opportunities and their priorities in your life. You will also learn how to determine which opportunities should be turned into projects.

Initiate (Step 2) – You will learn to get projects started by focusing on their charters and stakeholders.

Plan (Step 3) – You will learn to plan projects systematically. Step-by-step. The methodology discussed, once practiced by you again and again in the real world, should allow you to:

- **Plan small projects**, informally, with pen and paper, or in your head
- **Plan the work of larger projects** using a set of documented plans which can then be provided to the project team
- **Plan the management of work** using formal Project Management Plan documentation, which can help you professionally manage the project team

Implement (Step 4) – You will learn to delegate work, control work, and transition as work nears completion (we will not discuss how to do the actual work… that you will need to learn elsewhere, of course!).

Adapt (Step B) – You will learn to become more efficient and agile in planning and implementing projects. You will also learn how to handle multiple projects.

The **Deliverables** created while managing a project with this methodology are outlined in the diagrams in **Appendix C**. The **Activities** created while managing a project are presented in the diagrams in **Appendix D**.

Legal Disclaimer

Although the author and publisher made every effort to ensure that this book's information was accurate at press time, the author and publisher do not assume and hereby disclaim any liability to any party for any loss, damage, or disruption caused by errors or omissions.

The author and the publisher disclaim any and all liability to the maximum extent permitted by law if any information, analysis, opinions, advice, and/or recommendations in this book prove to be inaccurate, incomplete, unreliable, or result in any other losses.

The information contained in this book does not constitute legal, technical, or financial advice and should never be used without first consulting with legal and other professionals.

The publisher and the author do not make any guarantee or other promise as to any outcomes that may or may not be obtained from using this book's content. You should conduct your own research and due diligence.

About the Author

David Gadish, Ph.D., is a tenured university professor, a former management consultant, licensed real estate professional, real estate trainer, and coach.

David is a founding partner at Geffen Real Estate in Beverly Hills, California, where he oversees a team of residential and commercial real estate agents.

David is a professor at the College of Business and Economics, California State University, Los Angeles. He also currently teaches real estate at Touro College Los Angeles, a division of Touro University Worldwide, where he established the current real estate program.

David is also the author of several other books available on Amazon, including:

- "The Practical Guide to Career Opportunities in Real Estate: A Survey of Over 35 Careers with a Focus on Becoming an Excellent Real Estate Agent, with Introduction to Property Management, Real Estate Finance, Auctions, Leasing, Investing and 1031 Exchange".
- "The Eight Step Strategy for Success in Real Estate Sales: And The 18 Reasons Why Most New Real Estate Agents Fail, Featuring The 13 Key Factors in Selecting a Real Estate Brokerage".

In his spare time, David and his wife and business partner, Orit, raise their four daughters on their over 150 fruit tree orchard in Beverly Hills,

California. David Gadish can be reached via text at 310-433-0694 or via email at david@GeffenRealEstate.com.

Brief Table of Contents

Motivation 5

Overview 6

The UEIPIA Approach Introduced 6

Legal Disclaimer 8

About the Author 9

Table of Figures 25

Step A - Understand 26

Step A.1 - Understand Why You Can Accomplish Many More Goals in Your Life 28

Step A.2 - Understand Why Viewing Your Personal, Professional, and Business Life as A Set of Projects Will Benefit You 33

Step 1 – Evaluate 45

Step 1.1 - Compose a List of Projects You Are or Can be Working On ... 47

Step 1.2 - Define the Business Case for Each Project and Decide if to Proceed or Not 54

Step 2 – Initiate 66

Step 2.1 - Create the Project Charter Which Authorizes Your Project 68

Step 2.2 - Identify the Initial People (Stakeholders) Involved in Your Project 75

Step 3 – Plan 81

Step 3.1 - Define Your Project's Requirements and Scope 84

Step 3.2 - Detail Your Project's Deliverables and Activities 93

Step 3.3 - Determine Your Project's Schedule 117

Step 3.4 - Determine Your Project's Human Resource Requirements ... 128

Step 3.5 - Determine Your Project's Non-Human Resource Requirements 138

Step 3.6 - Determine Your Project's Costs and Budget 142

Step 3.7 - Determine the Risks Involved in Your Project and Responses to Them 149

Step 3.8 - Define Project Communication 159

Step 3.9 - Define Project Procurement 166

Step 3.10 - Define Stakeholder Engagement 171

Step 3.11 - Define the Quality of Project Deliverables and Activities 180

Step 3.12 - Plan Change Management 189

Step 3.13 - Plan Larger and/or More Formal Projects: The Project Management Plan 195

Step 4 – Implement 200

Step 4.1 - Delegate Work to Your Team 202

Step 4.2 - Perform Work on the Project's Activities 207

Step 4.3 - Control Your Project 209

Step 4.4 - Wrap Up the Project 217

Step B – Adapt 219

Step B.1 - Become More Efficient and Agile with Future Projects 221

Step B.2 - Juggle Multiple Projects at the Same Time 224

Appendixes 227

Appendix A - Drawing of a Fence Section 228

Appendix B - SCD Diet Plan 230

Appendix C – Project Management Related Deliverables Created When Managing a Project 231

Appendix D – Project Management Related Activities Performed When Managing a Project 234

Table of Contents

Contents

Motivation 5
Overview 6
The UEIPIA Approach Introduced 6
Legal Disclaimer 8
About the Author 9
Table of Figures 25
Step A - Understand 26
    Step A - Overview 27
    Step A - Outline 27
    Step A - Objectives 27
Step A.1 - Understand Why You Can Accomplish Many More Goals in Your Life 28
    Outline 28
    Introduction 28
    You Are Busy 29
    You Do Not Have Money 30
    You Do Not Have Time for Yourself 30
    You are Not Qualified to Evaluate Yourself 31
    You Need More and Less 31
Step A.2 - Understand Why Viewing Your Personal, Professional, and Business Life as A Set of Projects Will Benefit You 33
    Outline 33
    What is a Project? 34
    The Characteristics of Projects: 34

The Project Life Cycle 35
Additional Basic Definitions 38
Some Projects Have Multiple Phases 38
Where Do Projects Come From? 39
When Should Projects Be Handled? 39
Projects Come with Many Questions 39
Keys to Project Success 40
No Fear of the Unknown 41
Constantly Asking Questions 41
Your Role as a Project Manager 41
Are You Suggesting to Turn Every Little Task into a Project? 42

Step 1 – Evaluate 45
    Step 1 - Overview 46
    Step 1 - Outline 46
    Step 1 - Objectives 46
Step 1.1 - Compose a List of Projects You Are or Can be Working On 47
    Outline 47
    Introduction 47
    If You Have a Job 48
    If You Need a Job or are Looking for a Better Job 48
    If You Own a Business and Want to Grow It 49
    If You Want to Start a Business 50
    In Your Personal Life 51
    If You Are Single 52
    If You Are Married 52
    If You Have One or More Children 53

Step 1.2 - Define the Business Case for Each Project and Decide if to Proceed or Not 54

    Outline 54

    What's a Business Case? 54

    Why Create a Business Case? 55

    Case Studies – Creating a Business Case 55

    Perform a Cost-Benefit Analysis to include in your Business Case 59

    Case Studies – Cost-Benefit Analysis 60

    Conduct a Feasibility Study to Include in Your Business Case 61

    Case Studies – Feasibility Study 62

    Get Your Business Case Approved 63

    Case Studies – Project Approval 64

Step 2 – Initiate 66

    Step 2 - Overview 67

    Step 2 - Outline 67

    Step 2 - Objectives 67

Step 2.1 - Create the Project Charter Which Authorizes Your Project 68

    Outline 68

    What's a Project Charter? 68

    What is in the Project Charter? 68

    Why Create a Project Charter? 69

    Case Studies – Project Charter 69

Step 2.2 - Identify the Initial People (Stakeholders) Involved in Your Project 75

    Outline 75

    What's a Stakeholder? 75

    Why Create a List of Stakeholders? 75

    Create a List of Stakeholders 76

- Case Studies – List of Stakeholders 78
- More About Your Project's Stakeholders 80

Step 3 – Plan 81
- Step 3 - Overview 82
- Step 3 - Outline 82
- Step 3 - Objectives 83

Step 3.1 - Define Your Project's Requirements and Scope 84
- Outline 84
- Introduction 84
- Why Break Down the Requirements Further? 84
- How to Break Down the Requirements Further? 85
- Define Project Requirements 85
- Case Studies – Project Requirements 86
- What is Project Scope? 87
- Why is Defining Project Scope Important? 88
- What is Included in a Project Scope Statement? 88
- Case Studies – Project Scope 89

Step 3.2 - Detail Your Project's Deliverables and Activities 93
- Outline 93
- Why Break Down Your Projects into Parts? 93
- What is a Deliverable? 95
- What is an Activity? 95
- Rules for Breaking Down Deliverables or Activities Further 95
- The WBS Hierarchy 96
- WBS with Deliverables and Sub-Deliverables 97
- WBS with Deliverables, Sub-Deliverables, Activities, and Sub-Activities 98
- Draw a Diagram of Your Project's WBS 99

A Top-Down Approach to Creating Your WBS 100

A Bottom-Up Approach to Creating Your WBS 100

Case Studies – WBS with Deliverables and Sub-Deliverables Only (Chart Format) 101

Case Studies – WBS with Deliverables, Sub-Deliverables, Activities, Sub-Activities (List Format) 102

Case Studies – WBS with Deliverables, Sub-Deliverables, Activities, Sub-Activities (Chart Format) 114

Step 3.3 - Determine Your Project's Schedule 117

Outline 117

Introduction 117

What is a Milestone? 117

What is Activity Duration? 118

Estimate Activity Duration 118

Draw a Network Diagram 119

Case Studies – Network Diagram 120

Identify the Critical Path (Shortest Path) 122

Case Studies – Shortest Path Network Diagram 123

Project Schedule 125

Case Studies - Project Schedule 126

Step 3.4 - Determine Your Project's Human Resource Requirements 128

Outline 128

Introduction 128

What Makes Human Resources Great? 128

How to Find Great Human Resources? 129

Learn from Others about Your Project 131

Assign Human Resources to Activities 132

Human Resources for Larger Projects and or Organizations 132
Develop a Project Team 133
Human Resources Charts for Larger Projects 133
    Organizational Chart 134
    Responsibility Matrix 135
    Role Descriptions 136
Step 3.5 - Determine Your Project's Non-Human Resource Requirements 138
    Outline 138
    Introduction 138
    Categories of Non-Human Resources 138
    Initial Estimation of Non-Human Resources 139
    Detailed Estimation of Non-Human Resources 139
    Case Studies - Non-Human Resources 140
Step 3.6 - Determine Your Project's Costs and Budget 142
    Outline 142
    Why Estimate the Costs in More Detail? 142
    Should You Hide Revised Cost Estimates? 143
    How to Determine Cost of Human Resources? 143
    Case Studies – Cost of Human Resources 144
    How to Determine Cost of Non-Human Resources? 144
    Case Studies – Cost of Non-Human Resources 145
    Reserves 148
Step 3.7 - Determine the Risks Involved in Your Project and Responses to Them
.... 149
    Outline 149
    Why Focus on Risk? 149
    How to Identify Risks? 150

How to Record Risks? 150
Case Studies – Risk Identification 151
How to Assess Risks? 152
How to Record Risk Assessment? 153
Case Studies – Risk Assessment 153
How to Define Risk Responses? 155
How to Record Risk Responses? 156
Case Studies – Risk Responses 156

Step 3.8 - Define Project Communication 159
Outline 159
What is Communication? 159
Why Plan the Communication Related to Your Project? 159
The Communication Process 160
How is Communication Handled? 162
How Can Written Communication be Conducted? 162
How Frequently Should Communication Take Place? 163
Create a Communication Plan for Your Project 164
Case Studies – Communication Plan 164

Step 3.9 - Define Project Procurement 166
Outline 166
What Is Procurement? 166
Who is Involved in Procurement? 166
The Steps Involved in the Procurement Process 167
More About Procurement 168
Request for Quotation (RFQ) 168
Request for Proposal (RFP) 168
Request for Information (RFI) 169

- Inform Vendors About Your RFQ / RFP / RFI 169
- Receive and Evaluate Responses from Vendors 169
- Negotiate the Contract with Vendors and Assign Work 170

Step 3.10 - Define Stakeholder Engagement 171
- Outline 171
- Why is Engaging Stakeholders Important throughout Your Project? 171
- What's the Goal of Stakeholder Engagement Planning? 172
- Which Stakeholders Should be Engaged? 172
- Assess Stakeholder Power and Interest Level Before Planning Stakeholder Engagement 172
- Possible Engagement Statuses 173
- Document Current and Target Engagement Statuses 174
- Define When to Start Engaging Each Stakeholder 175
- Define How to Engage Each Stakeholder 175
- Define How Often to Engage Each Stakeholder 176
- Case Studies – Stakeholder Engagement Status 177

Step 3.11 - Define the Quality of Project Deliverables and Activities 180
- Outline 180
- What is Quality in the Context of Project Management? 180
- The Costs of Managing the Quality of the Activities and Deliverables of Your Project 181
- The Benefits of Managing the Quality of the Activities and Deliverables of Your Project 182
- What can you do to Increase the Quality of Your Project's Activities and Deliverables? 182
- The Quality Requirements for Your Project 183
- What is Quality Assurance? 184
- What is Quality Control? 184

What is Continuous Process Improvement? 185

Identify Quality Requirements.. 185

Create Quality Checklists 186

Define Quality Matrices 188

Step 3.12 - Plan Change Management 189

Outline... 189

Change Is All-Around 189

Why is it Important to Embrace Change Management During Projects? 190

What is Project Change Management? 190

Create an Environment Where Change is Welcome 191

Create a Formal Change Request Process... 191

Define the Change Request Form... 192

Define How Change Requests are Approved or Rejected 193

Step 3.13 - Plan Larger and/or More Formal Projects: The Project Management Plan 195

Outline... 195

Introduction 195

What is the Project Management Plan? 195

Should a Project Management Plan be Created?..................................... 196

When Should the Project Management Plan be Created? 196

Can a Project Management Plan be Modified Once Approved? 197

What is the Difference Between the Project Management Plan and all the Other Documents We Discussed So Far in this Book? 197

What Should be Included in the Project Management Plan? 198

Step 4 – Implement 200

Step 4 - Overview 201

Step 4 - Outline 201

- Step 4 - Objectives 201
- Step 4.1 - Delegate Work to Your Team 202
  - Outline 202
  - What is Authority, Responsibility, and Accountability? 202
  - What is Delegation? 203
  - Why Delegate? 203
  - What to Delegate? 203
  - To What Extent Can You Delegate? 204
  - How to Delegate? 204
  - How to Hold People Accountable When You Don't Have Direct Authority Over Them? 205
  - What Roles Can You Assign? 205
- Step 4.2 - Perform Work on the Project's Activities 207
  - Outline 207
  - When Should You Get the Work Started? 207
  - How to Inform Stakeholders That Work is Starting? 207
  - What to Do When Starting Work with Your Team? 207
- Step 4.3 - Control Your Project 209
  - Outline 209
  - What is Controlling a Project? 209
  - How to Control a Project? 209
  - Maintain Control by Tracking Progress 210
  - Maintain Control by Comparing Progress to Plans 211
  - Maintain Control Through Effective Change Request Management Procedures 211
  - Maintain Control Through Effective Communication to Minimize Conflict and Optimize Performance 212

- About Meetings 213
- Maintain Control Through Effective Leadership to Optimize Performance 214
- Key Characteristics of a Leader 214
- Why People Do What They Are Asked to Do? 215
- How Can you Establish Your Leadership? 215
- Maintaining Control Through Effective Stakeholder Engagement 216

Step 4.4 - Wrap Up the Project 217
- Outline 217
- Introduction 217
- Keep Your Team Focused to the End 217
- Help Stakeholders Transition 217
- Conduct a Post-Project Evaluation 218

Step B – Adapt 219
- Step B - Overview 220
- Step B - Outline 220
- Step B - Objectives 220

Step B.1 - Become More Efficient and Agile with Future Projects 221
- Outline 221
- Becoming Efficient with Future Projects 221
- Flexible (Agile) Approach to Project Management 221
- Frequent Update to Requirements 222
- Frequent Delivery of Subsets of the Final Deliverable 222
- Embracing Change Throughout the Project 222
- Embracing Increased Stakeholder Engagement Throughout the Project 223

Step B.2 - Juggle Multiple Projects at the Same Time 224
- Outline 224
- Introduction 224

  Coordinating Resources Across Projects 224

  Managing a Pipeline of Projects 225

  Delegating Project Management to Others 225

Appendixes 227

Appendix A - Drawing of a Fence Section 228

Appendix B - SCD Diet Plan 230

Appendix C – Project Management Related Deliverables Created When Managing a Project 231

Appendix D – Project Management Related Activities Performed When Managing a Project 234

Table of Figures

Figure 1 - The Characteristics of Projects 35
Figure 2 - The 6 Step Approach to Embracing Project Management 37
Figure 3 - Suggested Process for Gradually Adopting Project Management into Your Life 43
Figure 4 - Stakeholder Names and Roles 76
Figure 5 - Stakeholder Information 80
Figure 6 - Additional Stakeholder Information 80
Figure 7 - WBS Hierarchy Explained 97
Figure 8 – Sample WBS - Deliverables and Sub-Deliverables Only 98
Figure 9 - WBS Sample - Deliverables, Sub-Deliverables, Activities, and Sub-Activities .. 99
Figure 10 - Symbol Used to Redirect to Another Diagram 114
Figure 11 - The Process of Locating and Recruiting Human Resources 130
Figure 12 - Organization Chart 134
Figure 13 - The Communication Process 161
Figure 14 - The Fence Discussed in this Book 228
Figure 15 - Back of Fence (One Section) 229
Figure 16 - Key Deliverables Created When Managing a Project (Diagram 1 of 4) 232
Figure 17 - Key Deliverables Created When Managing a Project (Diagram 2 of 4) 232
Figure 18 - Key Deliverables Created When Managing a Project (Diagram 3 of 4) 233
Figure 19 - Key Deliverables Created When Managing a Project (Diagram 4 of 4) 233
Figure 20 - Key activities for each of the 6 steps discussed in this book 235

Step A - Understand

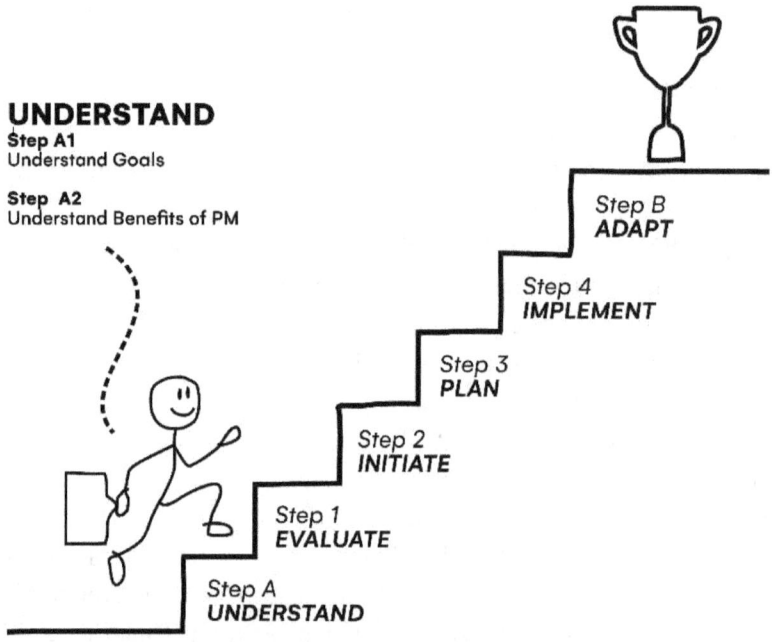

Step A - Overview

You will learn to better understand yourself, your goals, and the opportunities in your life. You will understand the benefits of bringing project management methodology into your professional, business, and personal life.

Step A - Outline

Step A.1 - Understand Why You Can Accomplish Many More Goals in Your Life

Step A.2 - Understand Why Viewing Your Personal, Professional, and Business Life as A Set of Projects Will Benefit You

Step A - Objectives

Objective A.1 – You should be able to self-reflect on, create a list of and prioritize your personal, professional, and business goals.

Objective A.2 - You should be able to explain the benefits of project management to personal, professional, and business success.

Step A.1 - Understand Why You Can Accomplish Many More Goals in Your Life

Outline

- You Are Busy
- You Do Not Have Money
- You Do Not Have Time for Yourself
- You are Not Qualified to Evaluate Yourself
- You Need More and Less

Introduction

My wife tells me often that I am wrong and that I need to apologize. So I apologize for what I am about to say next, but I have to say it just in case it may apply to you.

To be clear, I am sure what I am about to say next does not apply to you. You are better than that.

I figured I would start this book with some of the stories I heard from people, multiple people with the same stories, since I just can't get them out of my mind.

Again, I am sure these next few stories do not apply to you, so you can sadly lough about them with me… but just in case any of them do apply to you… maybe this is an excellent time to rethink a few things.

You Are Busy

You have Goals, but you will get started later. You are busy now doing something else. You have valid reasons for delaying. I understand.

You were in a car accident. Never your fault, of course. Got hit in the back again. Hurt your back. So you cannot think about making progress in your life for the next three months while you are recovering. I understand.

*****

Someone close to you, someone you know died, and you need to take a month off to recover. I am sorry for your loss. I understand. But why only a month? Maybe you need a year to recover while making sure you do not make progress with your own life?

*****

You need to take care of an older parent. I think you are a good human being for doing so. Here I am going on the record that when the time comes, I have no intention to send my and my wife's parents to a nursing home either. I understand. Taking care of them takes time. And, you have other commitments. But surely you can find some time to make progress with your own goals in between.

*****

You can't afford a vacation. I am sorry. At least you have money for McDonald's, and beer, and more fast food and maybe some slower food restaurants, and for processed foods full of poison. Have a drink, have a coke! Just do it! And eating and drinking all these terrible foods make you sleepy, so you need to watch TV and recover. I understand.

There must be more. You must have more reasons. Valid ones, of course, not to have time to take your life to the next level.

You Do Not Have Money

And then you also do not have enough money to get started with some of your goals. I understand and am sorry about your situation.

For eating fast food, restaurant food, processed foods, and coke full of chemicals that are nasty to your body, there is money, but to invest a bit in your future, there is none left. Makes total sense. I understand!

Maybe you just paid $200 for some collectible shoes, and you do not have money left to get some professional license. I understand.

You Do Not Have Time for Yourself

How many hours a day do you spend watching TV, movies, or other online programing? How many hours a day do you spend watching other people on social media? Can you spare some of that time to watch yourself as you handle life? More time for yourself, if spent efficiently on yourself, on your goals, can elevate you in many ways. Do you deserve more attention? Can you take half of that time for yourself? And if you see progress… maybe you will then take the other half for yourself as well. We will see.

You are Not Qualified to Evaluate Yourself

You are active on social media… You like people, photos, videos, articles, and more… so you click LIKE and even LOVE (often it's political). And if you do not like it, you keep scrolling down. You are busy reviewing people's lives, providing them feedback. You have become a judge and jury!

Can you take half of that time for self-review and reflection? And if you see progress… maybe you will then take the other half for yourself as well. We will see.

You Need More and Less

You see that more time and some money is around you, available for you to grab. Will you? All that is needed to get there are fewer excuses.

But more time with no effective way to capitalize on it may lead back to wasted time. So let's look at a strategy of what you can do with all that extra time you have.

This strategy will also help you do the many positive things you do in your life more efficiently so that you can have even more free time to do more positive things, and yes, also have more time to get some rest.

Remember the goals that you were going to leave for later. Well, now you have time for some of them. But how do you go about achieving them? Some are big and overwhelming to think about. You may want to find an amazing human being to get married to. You might want to find a beautiful home to purchase to live in. You might want to start a business, turn it into a success and quit your job, and on and on.

One way to look at achieving your goals, no matter how complex they may appear to be, is by systematically turning them into projects and systematically managing them.

But how? There is a whole professional field of Project Management. It's a bit complex, but I will simplify it for you in this book so you can incorporate the "system of managing your personal, professional, and or business life as a bunch of projects" in the various facets of your life and then use it to elevate yourself to be able to achieve those dreams and goals of yours you were going to pursue later… sooner.

So, let's get started with some basics about projects and project management.

Step A.2 - Understand Why Viewing Your Personal, Professional, and Business Life as A Set of Projects Will Benefit You

Outline

- What is a Project?
- The Characteristics of Projects
- The Project Life Cycle
- Additional Basic Definitions
- Some Projects Have Multiple Phases
- Where Do Projects Come From?
- When Should Projects Be Handled?
- Projects Come with Many Questions
- Keys to Project Success
- No Fear of the Unknown
- Constantly Asking Questions
- Your Role as a Project Manager
- Are You Suggesting to Turn Every Little Task into a Project?

What is a Project?

A **Project** is a temporary effort undertaken to create a specific product, service, **DIK** (Data, Information, Knowledge), or result. A project is a temporary endeavor and has a specific start date and time and end date and time. It also has a defined scope and specific resources assigned to accomplish it.

This definition is critical to understand, so let me go over it again, this time as a list of bullets.

The Characteristics of Projects:

A project's characteristics include:

- Specific goal to achieve
- Temporary in nature (start and end)
- Specific scope of what to do to achieve the goal
- Specific human resources assigned to achieve it (for example, you need Linda and Jose to help you with the project)
- Specific non-human resources assigned to achieve it (for example, you need a cell phone and a laptop, or a shovel)

And let me show you a visualization of the characteristics of projects (see Figure 1 below):

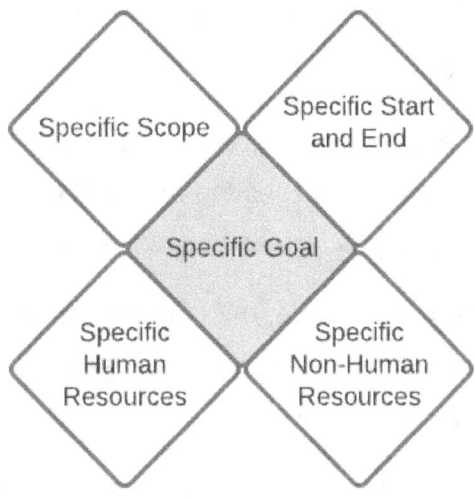

Figure 1 - The Characteristics of Projects

The Project Life Cycle

A project starts with a goal, an idea, or a dream. The goal, vision, or dream can be yours or someone else's. You can work on your own projects or on those of others.

A Business Case document is created in more formal projects as part of an initial evaluation of a possible project. If a blessing is given to proceed, a **Project Charter** document is formed next, providing more information and clarity about the project's direction.

If approved, the project continues with a planning phase. In a more formal project, you create various **Planning Documents**. In the most formal projects, you also create a **Project Management Plan**.

Once the plans are good enough, **Work** begins, as is the **Control** of the work by the project manager (you can do the work and manage yourself in smaller projects). In more formal projects, you end up with a **Final Deliverable**.

You can end the project there, but in more formal projects, a deliverable does not end the project since you spend time learning lessons and finalizing **Documentation** related to the project.

The following diagram (Figure 2) visualizes the six steps of my approach to embracing project management. You start with step A and end up in step B. To get there, you also go through Steps 1,2,3, and 4 which are the four core steps of managing an actual project:

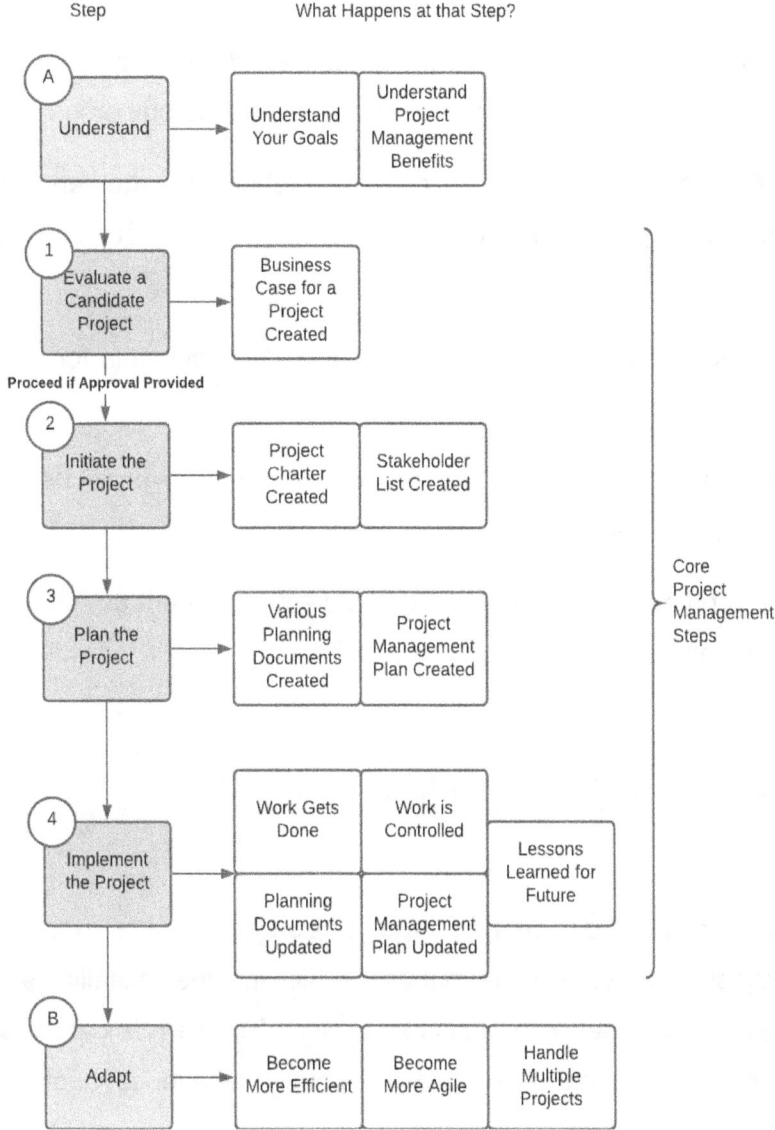

Figure 2 - The 6 Step Approach to Embracing Project Management

Additional Basic Definitions

A **Project Owner** is the person that initiates the project, finances it, and is in charge of it. The project owner is also likely to own the outcomes of the project.

A **Project Sponsor** is typically in higher management at a larger organization. They provide the approval for projects and resources to accomplish them.

A **Project Manager,** on the other hand, is responsible for all aspects of the project.

You may be the project owner, project manager, project sponsor, or a combination of the three.

The good news is that managing a project is different than having to do all the work yourself.

Some Projects Have Multiple Phases

It is up to you how small or large your project is. For example, you can define a project to redevelop your front yard, which includes installing a new fence, new irrigation system, new sod, and landscaping. You can look at the same work as a set of smaller projects: one project to install a new fence, another project to install a new irrigation system, and so on.

And then, you can look at the work as one project that consists of multiple phases. Phase one of the project – install a new fence, phase two of the project – install a new irrigation system, and so on.

No matter how you choose to look at the work, you will still be able to apply all the project management-related lessons you will learn in this book.

Where Do Projects Come From?

Projects can come from you. You can turn problems in your personal, professional, or business life into projects. You can turn opportunities into projects as well!

Projects can also come from others. They can come from your husband/wife, partner, child, friend, client, supplier, or anyone/anywhere else.

When Should Projects Be Handled?

When you dream of a new project, ask yourself if it should be handled in the near future or not. If not, place your idea in the "Future Projects" bucket in your To-Do list. You will get back to it when you can, as well as when you periodically review this "Future Projects" bucket.

Projects Come with Many Questions

Often when you get started on a project, you have no idea how long it will take to complete. You may have many questions, such as what are the project's goal(s)? Who will help you? What exactly needs to be done to accomplish the goal(s)? How much time do you have? Need? What resources do you need?

You likely want to do a good job managing the project. What do you need to do to successfully manage the project and achieve the project's goal(s)?

Keys to Project Success

Success as a project manager requires many things. Key among them are:

- No fear of the unknown
- Constantly asking questions
- Understanding how to manage projects
- Acting when action is called for
- Working to understand the big picture
- Uncovering the details that make up the big picture
- Making realistic assumptions and estimating based on them
- Surrounding yourself with the right people
- Communicating clearly with people
- Leading people

We will discuss these further throughout the book.

No Fear of the Unknown

We do not know much about the world we live in. We do not know what the next moment will bring. We do not know who will enter or who will exit our lives, and on and on and on.

What's the point of being afraid of what we do not know?

Constantly Asking Questions

Successful people do not have time to be afraid of the unknown. They spend their time asking questions about the unknown and then seeking answers.

For example, most people will never write a book. This is my third one. I treat them as projects. I had a project with a goal and no clue how to achieve the goal. I did not know how to write books, so I asked myself: How do I write books? What are the steps? What is an acceptable format for this type of book? How to publish a book, how to get an ISBN, and more and more questions. I then went looking for answers. I bought books on how to write books! I got answers.

Your Role as a Project Manager

Your role as a project manager may consist of the following aspects:

- Determine (or help determine) if to proceed with a project
- Define the project at a high level

- Develop detailed work plans for the project
- Develop a management plan for the project (mainly for more complex and or more formal projects)
- Delegate the work (if you have a team)
- Do the work (for some projects), have others do the work (for other projects)
- Monitor and control the work (this may include monitoring and controlling yourself). This includes handling informal or formal change requests
- Learn lessons, and transition to other things

Are You Suggesting to Turn Every Little Task into a Project?

No and Yes. Let me explain. I suggest you do the following (See Figure 3):

1. Continue reading the book to learn the process. Highlight key points as you go.
2. Reread the book if needed, focusing on the key points you highlighted previously.
3. Apply the process to one project that you believe could take one week to one month to complete. Do not start with a very small project that may take a few hours since applying the process to a project the first time will take so long you may not see the benefit in all the "extra" work.
4. Apply the process to one or more other projects of a similar magnitude (projects that may take one week to one month to complete).
5. Once you learn the process, you can apply it to larger and larger projects.

6. Once the process is engrained in your head and heart, you will see that you start applying it without thinking and without much overhead to very small projects that take a few minutes, a few hours, or a few days.

This recommended process is illustrated in Figure 3 below.

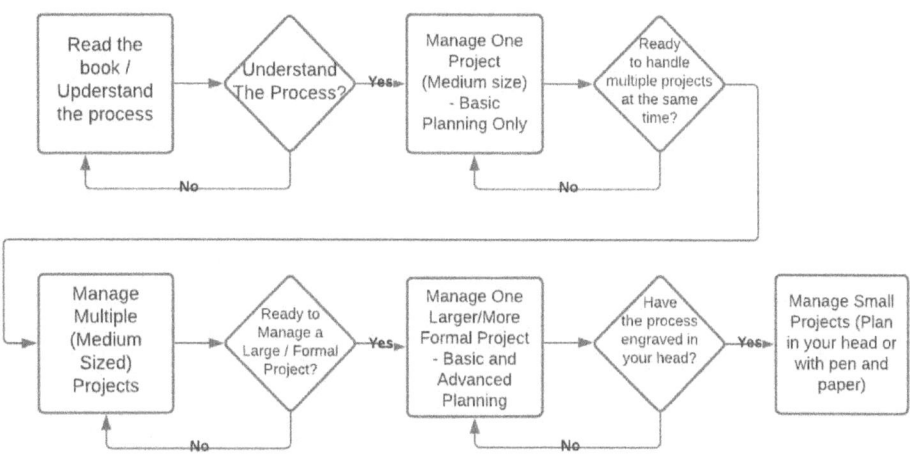

Figure 3 - Suggested Process for Gradually Adopting Project Management into Your Life

I am at a stage in my life where I look at (almost?) everything as a project. For example, as I was writing this paragraph, I was sitting in our backyard farm. An inspiring location to write. Inspiring and quiet. Suddenly I heard some screaming and crying, and my wife and four daughters came towards me. I asked my wife why they were screaming and crying. She told me, "they all want my individual attention". I informed my daughters that I will schedule four half-hour sessions with mom—asked the youngest to go first and hang with my wife on the trampoline while the other three play hide and seek in the farm. I was now working on two projects at the same time. Writing this book and coordinating four half-hour "play time with mom" sessions. Everyone was quiet, and I was able to write for 28 more minutes. At that time, I switched projects and called another daughter to replace the first one at the trampoline with mom. I then switched back to continuing to write the book… Two hours passed this way. My four daughters and wife were happy, and I got two hours of mostly quiet time to make progress with this book. Projects!

Step 1 – Evaluate

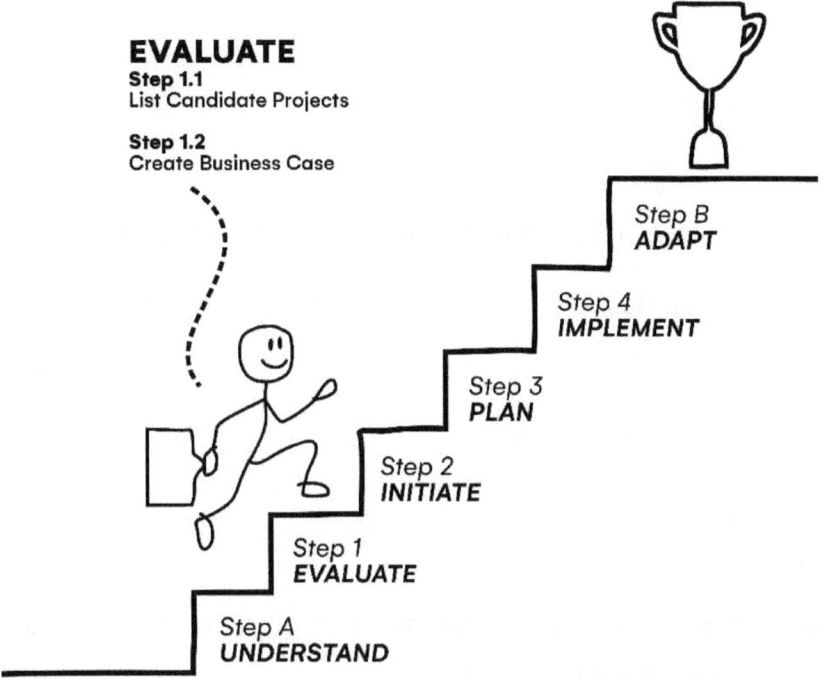

Step 1 - Overview

You will learn to evaluate the opportunities and their priorities in your life. You will also learn how to determine which opportunities should be turned into projects.

Step 1 - Outline

Step 1.1 - Compose a List of Projects You Are or Can be Working On

Step 1.2 - Define the Business Case for Each Project and Decide if to Proceed or Not

Step 1 - Objectives

You should be able to create prioritized lists of candidate projects in your personal, professional, and business endeavors.

You should be able to create a business case for a possible project and ask for its approval.

Step 1.1 - Compose a List of Projects You Are or Can be Working On

Outline

>If You Have a Job
>
>If You Need a Job or are Looking for a Better Job
>
>If You Own a Business and Want to Grow It
>
>If You Want to Start a Business
>
>In Your Personal Life
>
>If You Are Single
>
>If You Are Married
>
>If You Have One or More Children

Introduction

An idea for a project can arise from a need you or someone else recognizes, from a problem you or someone else is trying to solve, or an opportunity you or someone else encounters.

In the remainder of this section, we will look at possible projects that may or may not apply to your situation. I encourage you to use them as a starting point to create your own list(s) of possible projects. For some projects below, I provide specific examples to further trigger your imagination.

If you are already working on some of these – fantastic! You can still turn them into more formal projects using the methodology I present in this book.

If You Have a Job

If you have a job, possible projects include:

- Learn a new skill (e.g., learn to bake a cake)
- Get a professional license (e.g., take courses and pass the state exam to get a real estate license)
- Get formal training (e.g., ask your manager to allow you to attend a business communication workshop)
- Get informal training (e.g., learn from a colleague how to perform a new task)
- Attend a conference
- Ask for a promotion
- Ask for increased pay
- Quit your job (I am not telling you to quit your job!)

If You Need a Job or are Looking for a Better Job

Possible projects include:

- Research career options (e.g., buy one of my books on career opportunities in real estate by searching my name on Amazon, read them, and decide if a career in real estate is for you... ☺)
- Create a resume and cover letter
- Learn to interview
- Apply to advertised positions

If You Own a Business and Want to Grow It

As a business owner, there are many things you need to do to establish and then maintain your success in the face of fierce competition. Possible projects include:

- Evaluate your business
- Determine your business development strategy
- Create and maintain a website
- Create and maintain a social media presence
- Create marketing materials to promote your business, your brand, your products and or services, and or DIK
- Write an article
- Market an article you wrote
- Network in a specific organization
- Meet with a lead (potential client)
- Convert a lead to a paying client
- Follow-up with past clients
- Work on a holiday marketing campaign

- Attend a conference
- Sell your business
- Pass your business to a family member
- Shut your business down

If You Want to Start a Business

Projects could include the following:

- Research different business sectors/business options (did I mention I love real estate? But remember this… great opportunities are awaiting you in any business sector if you cannot wait to get started and will never give up)
- Create a business plan
- Apply for a business loan
- Lease/purchase real estate for the business
- Get formal training (e.g., become a certified nutritionist)
- Attend a conference (to get ideas on various businesses and network with people)

Additionally, you need to handle a multitude of additional things in your life. We look at them next.

In Your Personal Life

Life keeps you busy. Your life may benefit from many or all of the following possible projects:

- Learn to eat healthily
- Find where to shop online (I used to spend half of each Sunday dragging my family shopping. We now shop exclusively online).
- Shop online.
- Plan and go on vacation
- Lose weight
- Join a health club
- Learn to play some competitive sport
- Define what TV shows you plan to watch this season
- Spend the weekend with your family
- Go out with friends
- Go shopping
- Attend an entertainment or sporting event
- Pet-related activities
- Buy a house
- Fix your house

Did I mention shopping online? I finally took it upon myself to learn to shop online (at the start of COVID-19). My wife, Orit (her name is pronounced as "Or-Eat"... as in "drink or eat"!), and I spent years taking our kids shopping each Sunday. Shopping for groceries, clothing, and so on. We would pack food for the day, get the kids into the SUV, drive to Costco, this supermarket, that supermarket, this store, and that store. The kids would get hungry at random times, need the restroom, get upset with one another or just be bored. We would come home at two, three, and sometimes four pm. We were exhausted. The day was practically over—what a waste. We finally discovered online shopping. The first days and weeks of online shopping were rough. But I looked at the experience as a project whose goal it was for me to become efficient at online shopping.

I am now at a stage where I may spend no more than 30 min on food and other household shopping per week, and my wife may spend another 1-2 hours per month shopping for clothing and other items online (translates to no more than 30 min a week). Thus we each freed up our hole Sunday! More time to spend with the kids, more time to relax, more time to write books (check out David Gadish, as well as Orit Gadish on Amazon!), and more time to handle real estate deals! What a deal!

If You Are Single

If you are single, possible projects (in addition to those listed in the previous section) include:

- Find a husband/wife
- Get married

If You Are Married

If you are married, possible projects include:

- Have a baby
- Work on resolving any issues between you and your husband/wife

If You Have One or More Children

If you have one or more children, possible projects include:

- Find them the best schools to attend
- Work to get them closer to you
- Take care of them when sick
- Help with math or another subject
- Filter their friends and determine who they should keep
- Save money for their university education
- Buy them gifts for the holidays
- Teach them how to ride a bike
- Help them plan and have a wedding (when they grow up)

You can treat any of these ideas as projects and work systematically to make them happen! But not so quick. You should start slow. Pick one possible project and move on to the next step with it. Eventually, once you understand the process and have practiced it on one project at a time, you can venture to manage multiple projects at a time.

Step 1.2 - Define the Business Case for Each Project and Decide if to Proceed or Not

Outline

- What's a Business Case?
- Why Create a Business Case?
- Case Studies – Creating a Business Case
- Perform a Cost-Benefit Analysis to include in your Business Case
- Case Studies – Cost-Benefit Analysis
- Conduct a Feasibility Study to Include in Your Business Case
- Case Studies – Feasibility Study
- Get Your Business Case Approved
- Case Studies – Project Approval

What's a Business Case?

The initial information describing a proposed project is often presented in a Business Case. The Business Case is a document (you can write it using MSWord) that helps you or someone else (project owner or project sponsor) decide if to proceed with a proposed project on not. It may contain but is not limited to some or all of the following:

- Name of the project (preliminary)
- Reason(s) the project is needed

- Benefit(s) the project will provide
- Statement of personal, professional, or business problem or opportunity the project will deal with
- The people affected by the problem or opportunity (stakeholders)
- Scope of the proposed project (preliminary) – what will be and what will not be included in the project
- The deadline for completing the project (estimated) - can be the length of time from the start (e.g., complete in three weeks) or a specific date
- Costs involved in the project (estimated) – both human labor costs and non-human labor costs (e.g., buy a laptop, subscribe to an online website, buy a shovel to dig holes, etc.)
- Risks involved in not proceeding with the project – what could happen if the proposed project is not approved (e.g., if you do not install a fence, your children can run to the street and get into an accident)
- Risks involved in proceeding with the project – what can happen if the project is approved and work starts (e.g., you can injure your back while digging holes in the ground)

Why Create a Business Case?

The business case is presented to those with the money to fund it. You can present it to yourself! You can present it to your wife or husband, to your manager, or an investor, or anyone else.

Case Studies – Creating a Business Case

We will discuss two real-world projects throughout much of this book. The first example has to do with building a fence (Fence Project). The second example showcases a project to determine if a specific diet can help an infant's serious medical condition (SCD for Life Project). You are welcome to follow one or both projects, depending on your interest in the topic.

I selected these two real-world examples from my life that are not trivial yet not overly complex to explain. I hope that these examples will help you gain clarity on the project management process and be memorable. You can then utilize the process outlined in this book for more complex projects. Finally, once the process of managing projects is engrained in you, you might be able to apply this process to very small projects in your head without the need for detailed, time-consuming documentation or with handwritten documentation you put together using pen on paper in a matter of minutes.

I believe that some planning is better than no planning… if your planning is done property. Let's start with showing you a possible business case for each of these two projects:

Fence Project – Business Case

Motivation (Reason) for Project: I have young kids and do not want them to run to the street. We live in the hills, as do the coyotes. I want to keep the coyotes away from the kids and the kids away from the street. There are currently 10ft high bushes separating the front yard and the street, but there are some gaps between them. The fence will be located behind the bushes such that when looking at the property from the street, you will see the bushes first and portions of the fence behind the bushes (see Appendix A for a drawing of the fence).

People Affected (Stakeholders):
- David (Me)
- Orit (My wife)
- My four young children
- My neighbor(s)

Scope of Project:

Build a 200ft long fence at the front of the property. The fence will be wooden, 6ft tall. The two gates, one leading to the front of the house and the other to the driveway leading to the garage, already exist and are therefore outside of this project's scope.

Deadline for Project Completion:

No firm deadline, but ideally want to finish as soon as possible in about 2-3 weeks would be great.

SCD for Life Project – Business Case

Motivation (Reason) for Project: My daughter started bleeding (internally) at the age of 4 months (and we observed blood in her stool), and by the time she was about to turn one, she was so weak and thin, she could barely move. For eight months, we took her to tens of doctors and consulted with tens of other doctors (phone consultations), but they misdiagnosed her and proposed solutions that, in retrospect, may have caused more damage to her. Finally, a colonoscopy/endoscopy at Cedar Sinai Medical Center in Los Angeles determined this was likely Crohn's. She was hospitalized at UCLA Medical

Center. With advice from a Harvard professor, local doctors advised that the only option was to give her steroids and other drugs. We were told she would need to take them for life. When we asked about side effects, we were told they could lead to cancer. We also read research that over 50% of babies with this condition do not make it. We agreed to proceed with medications but stopped after three months once she stabilized and regained weight. She started bleeding again, so we had to find a different solution. We looked at Chinese medicine but gave up on it after a three-month trial. We looked at a vegan diet that claimed to work for Crohn's patients but gave up on that too after two months, having seen no progress. We finally discovered a book on Amazon about the **Specific Carbohydrate Diet (SCD)** diet. The author was a professor of pediatrics and practices at the Seattle Children's Hospital. Orit called his office and left him a message. He called her back and directed her to a Facebook group of mothers whose children are on this diet. This was the start of Orit's SCD for Life Project to save our daughter. You can find out more about the SCD diet in **Appendix B** of this book.

People Affected (Stakeholders):
- My daughter
- Orit
- My other three daughters
- Me

Scope of Project:
Try the SCD Diet and see if it works for our daughter.

Deadline for Project Completion:

> As soon as possible.
>
> Risks in Proceeding:
> - SCD Diet will fail
> - Continued weight loss
> - Continued internal bleeding (see blood in stool)
>
> Risks in Not Proceeding:
> - We will need to keep looking for another alternative food-based management of our daughter's Crohn's.
> - We will need to get her back on medication that may result in cancer.

In the examples above, I was the Project Owner of the Fence Project (I decided we should have a fence), and Orit was the Project Owner of the SCD Diet Project (she decided she wants to find a food-based alternative to handling Crohn's in babies). To be clear, my wife Orit and I did not create two formal documents presenting business cases to one another. We also did not create the other documents discussed in this book. Why? Like myself, Orit had extensive corporate experience. At one point, she served as a manager of a team of project managers. This allowed both of us to manage these and other projects that are of smaller scope, systematically partially in our heads and partly using pen on paper.

Perform a Cost-Benefit Analysis to include in your Business Case

Cost-Benefit Analysis should be performed as part of developing your project charter. Determine the various benefits likely from your project. Determine the different costs connected to initiating, planning, and implementing your project. Compare the two.

Note that for many projects, benefits can last for a long time, as can the costs, so these need to be accounted for as well.

Performing a simple cost-benefit analysis can help you with three important things:

- It helps decide if to proceed with the project or not (if the costs outweigh the benefits, it may not be worthwhile to proceed with the project).
- It helps you develop project success measures (you will have an idea at a high level of what it means to be successful).
- It helps you estimate resources required for the project (you will have a high-level estimate of the human and non-human costs involved in implementing the project).

Case Studies – Cost-Benefit Analysis

Fence Project – Cost-Benefit Analysis

Costs:
Material and tool costs of about $2,500 (I called Home Depot and Lowes and determined that cost of materials per SF is about $10, and since I have 200SF frontage, the materials would be about $200. Add to that $500 for tools, nails, etc.)

No labor costs as I will do the job. Benefits: increased security for my children and the whole family.
SCD for Life Project – Cost-Benefit Analysis Estimated Costs: - Cost of food - Cost of kitchen equipment to prepare food (if not available) Less than $100 for the 3-day long phase 0 of the diet. If this initial phase of the project is a success, Additional costs of about $100 per week for life Kitchen equipment – one time $100 Benefits: Save my daughter's life!

Conduct a Feasibility Study to Include in Your Business Case

Conducting a feasibility study will help you achieve three goals:

- Determine if the project can be accomplished
- Determine if the results of the project can provide a benefit
- Determine if the project can provide a reasonable approach to its goals and objectives

To determine the project's feasibility, focus on the following five areas:

- **Operational Feasibility** – how likely are the results to satisfy your or your organization's needs?
- **Technical Feasibility** - do you have, or can you acquire, the technical resources, including people, equipment, facilities materials, and DIK, to bring the project to a successful conclusion?
- **Financial Feasibility** – Do you have the funds to acquire all that is needed to bring the project to a conclusion on time?
- **Time Feasibility** - Can you conclude the project on time given available funds?
- **Legal Feasibility** - are there any laws that would prevent you from completing the project as planned?

Case Studies – Feasibility Study

Fence Project – Feasibility Study

- Operational Feasibility – The fence will provide the needed privacy and security
- Technical Feasibility – I will do the work. Materials appear to be available to purchase – some at Home Depot and others in Lowes.
- Financial Feasibility – I have the funds needed to purchase the materials and tools
- Time Feasibility – The project can be concluded in the time frame discussed
- Legal Feasibility – The fence cannot be taller than 6ft, which is fine given this is the size of our proposed fence

I could have built an 8-ft section of the fence as part of a feasibility study to establish if I can build the fence, but I decided to just go for it and build the whole fence.
SCD for Life Project – Feasibility Study Feasibility Study: Proceed with phase 0 of the SCD diet. If we see promising results in phase 0, continue with the diet. So, in a way, this project in itself is a feasibility study for additional projects (to implement future phases of the SCD diet). • Operational Feasibility – We do not know if the results will satisfy our needs. We plan to proceed with phase 0 of the SCD diet. If we see promising results in phase 0, we will continue with the diet's subsequent phases. • Technical Feasibility – We can acquire knowledge about the SCD diet online, and we can purchase the food via online shopping. • Financial Feasibility – The cost of food is minor. We can afford it. • Time Feasibility – We want to conclude phase 0 of the SCD diet asap so we can determine if it works and proceed with the other phases if it does. • Legal Feasibility – No laws would prevent us from proceeding with the project

Get Your Business Case Approved

Now that your business case is complete, take a look at the document again. It is always a good idea to review your documents multiple times before providing them to others. This is your opportunity to uncover and resolve any spelling, grammar, logic and other issues. It will increase the chances of getting your business case approved by others.

Provide the business case document to those that are in a position to approve the project and/or provide you with funding to proceed with the project. Consider a combination of emailing them a soft copy, meeting with them in person or via zoom, providing a hard copy. A presentation of your business case could be informal or highly formal given who the stakeholders are and the situation.

If the approval is immediate – Great! If they need time to review, suggest a deadline. With more formal projects, get the required signatures to make the approval official.

Hope your project gets approved! If not, don't give up and keep going with others.

Case Studies – Project Approval

I shared my project's findings with Orit, and she shared her project's findings with me. We decided as follows:

Fence Project – Project Approval

Action: Proceed to get Orit's blessing to get started without a feasibility study since I believed I could do it. Decision: Orit agreed we needed the fence and was ok with spending the money necessary for the materials. I told her that I would get a better idea of the costs and let her know.

SCD for Life Project – Project Approval Action: decide if to proceed to feasibility study (that is, proceed to implement phase 0 of the diet and see if it works for our baby). Decision: We met for two minutes. Orit told me about the diet and that she wants to try it. How could I refuse? So, she got started right away by learning some more about the diet and sharing that with me.

If a project is approved, a Project Charter should be created for the project as a next step. It can be created by you, the project manager that will be assigned to the project, or anyone else tasked with the work.

Step 2 – Initiate

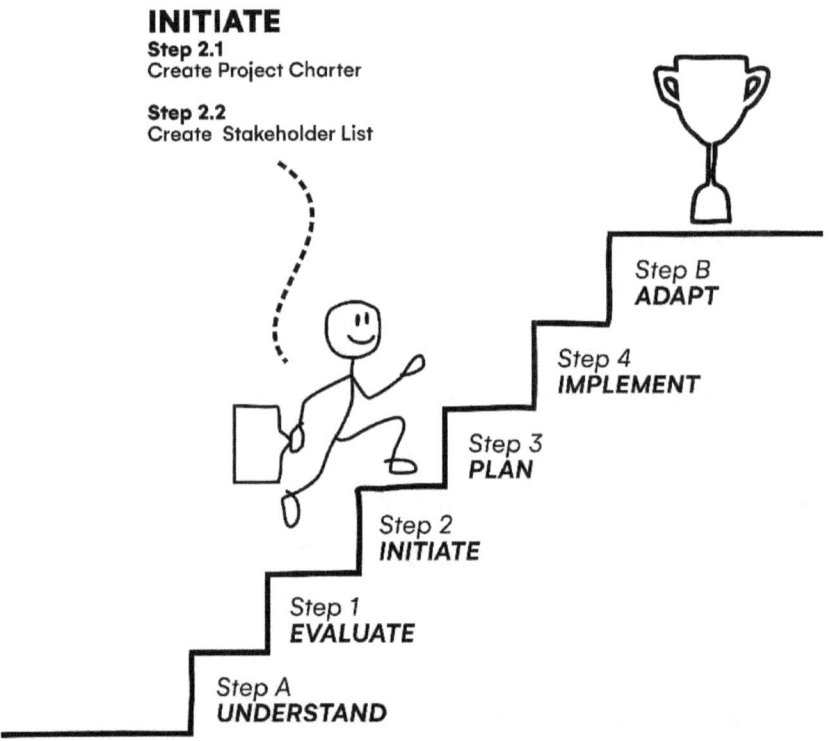

Step 2 - Overview

You will learn to get projects started by focusing on their charters and stakeholders.

Step 2 - Outline

Step 2.1 - Create the Project Charter Which Authorizes Your Project

Step 2.2 - Identify the Initial People (Stakeholders) Involved in Your Project

Step 2 - Objectives

You should be able to create a Project Charter document for a specific project.

You should be able to create a Stakeholder Register for a specific project.

Step 2.1 - Create the Project Charter Which Authorizes Your Project

Outline

> What's a Project Charter?
> What is in the Project Charter?
> Why Create a Project Charter?
> Case Studies – Project Charter

What's a Project Charter?

Project Charter is a document that formally authorizes the project and provides the project manager (you) with authority to use financial and other resources to achieve project goals.

What is in the Project Charter?

The project charter's components typically include the following:

- **Goals** - what you want to achieve, a higher-level statement of desired results (for example: build a new product, create a new service, increase income, decrease costs, etc.)

- **Objectives** - specific, measurable outcomes (for example: increase income by 20% in 6 months, cut expenses by 10% within two months)
- **High-Level Requirements** – conditions the project needs to meet. Not detailed requirements, those come later during project planning
- **Key Milestones and Dates** - specific points in time in the project's schedule used to measure the project's progress as the project progresses towards achieving its goals
- Overview of human project costs
- Overview of non-human resource project costs
- Overview of project risk
- Project participants (initial stakeholder list)
- Assigned project manager (maybe you!)
- Project Sponsor/owner (maybe also you!)

Why Create a Project Charter?

The **Project Charter** document builds on the Business Case document, and there will be some duplication of information.

Is it possible to proceed to the next step without creating a project charter? Yes. So why spend the time creating it? Because it allows you to take a bit of time and answer important questions about the project that will create further clarity for you and everyone else that will be involved.

Case Studies – Project Charter

Below are examples of possible Project Charter documents for the two projects we are following in this book:

Fence Project – Project Charter

Goals:
- Build a 6 ft wooden fence, 200 ft long

Objectives:
- Do it with as little money as possible
- Do it within 4-5 weeks (so I can move to do other projects around the house).

High-Level Requirements
- It is required for me to watch YouTube videos to learn how to build a wood fence
- It is required for me to discuss with professionals how they do it
- It is required for me to create a list of materials needed
- It is required for me to create a list of equipment needed
- It is required for me to purchase materials for the fence
- It is required for me to purchase equipment to build the fence

Key Milestones Dates
- Start January 1
- Materials and tools at the property – Jan 14
- Holes for posts dug every 8 ft – Jan 21
- All posts set in concrete – Feb 1

- All fence rails installed utilizing fence rail brackets – Feb 4
- All pickets hammered to the rails – Feb 18
- Fence painted – Feb 22
- Site cleaned up – Feb 23

Human Resource Costs:

No HR cost if I handle myself and do the work at times when I usually rest (rest for me is working in my backyard farm).

Non-Human Resource Costs:

I went to HomeDepot.com and found materials to be about $2,2000 and $300 for tools.

Risks:
- Materials will not be available when I need them
- Material delivery will be delayed
- Additional costs I did not think of
- Injury during construction

Participants:
- David (Me)
- Home Depot

Project Manager:
- David

Project Sponsor/owner:

- Orit

SCD for Life Project – Project Charter

Goals:
- Help my daughter live a reasonably healthy life with Crohn's, without medications if possible

Objectives:
- Determine if the SCD diet is a viable option to reduce my daughter's internal inflammation and bleeding
- Determine this as quickly as possible within days but no longer than within weeks.

High-Level Requirements:
- It is required to understand the SCD diet better (See Appendix B, and follow the link to find out more about it on the web if you have not yet done so… It will help you better understand this case study we follow throughout the book!)
- It is required to research variations of the SCD diet and decide on a specific approach to stage 0 of that diet
- It is required to purchase food that is compatible with the SCD diet stage 0
- It may be required to buy kitchen equipment to prepare stage 0 food (if the equipment is not available in our home)
- It is required to prepare SCD stage 0 food
- It is required to feed our baby stage 0 food

- It is required to monitor her stool to determine if the internal bleeding stops
- If it does stop, it will be required to proceed to stages 1, then 2, 3, 4, and finally 5 (but this is outside the scope of this initial project)

Key Milestones and Dates:
- Specific food and quantities to order are established
- Food is ordered Online
- Food is Delivered (same day – www.instacart.com)
- Cooking equipment is found or ordered online
- Cooking equipment is delivered (next day – www.amazon.com)
- Food preparation ends – the same day as food and equipment delivered or the next day at the latest
- Stage 0 ends – 3 days after food preparation ends

Human Resource Costs:
- Orit - time to read SCD book, consult other mothers on the SCD Facebook page, and make food
- David – time to review findings with Orit
- David – time to cut anything that needs to be cut with a knife (prep work)
- Orit – time to cook the food
- David – Time to place the dirty dishes in the dishwasher
- David – Time to move clean dishes out of the dishwasher and back on the shelves
- Orit – time to feed the baby
- David – time to feed the baby

Non-Human Resource Costs:
- The extra cost of food - $100/week
- InstaPot purchase - $100

Risks:
- Bleeding will not stop
- Bleeding with an increase in frequency and quantity

Participants:
- Orit
- David
- Baby daughter
- Sisters - our three other daughters

Project Manager:
- Orit

Project Sponsor:
- Orit
- David

Step 2.2 - Identify the Initial People (Stakeholders) Involved in Your Project

Outline

> What's a Stakeholder?
> Why Create a List of Stakeholders?
> Create a List of Stakeholders
> Case Studies – List of Stakeholders
> More About Your Project's Stakeholders

What's a Stakeholder?

A **Stakeholder** is any person or group that supports, is affected by, or is interested in your project (not a Steak holder!). Stakeholders can be internal to your organization or external to it.

Why Create a List of Stakeholders?

Knowing who these people are, allows you to plan to involve them at the appropriate times during your project. You should record their names as well as the **Roles** you expect them to play. Remember, things change all the time. People will move in and out of your list. Their roles will change as you refine your understanding of your project and your understanding of these people.

Create a List of Stakeholders

At this stage, you can create a list of the stakeholders. The Project Stakeholders list looks like this (See Figure 4).

Stakeholder Role	Stakeholder Name

Figure 4 - Stakeholder Names and Roles

For a personal project, stakeholders can be:

- You
- Family members
- Friends
- Neighbors
- Government
- A certain group of people
- A certain team of people
- The public

For a professional project for an organization you work for, stakeholders can be:

- You
- Upper management
- Project manager (if other than yourself)
- Your team's members
- Another team's members (if you are playing a professional sport, for example)
- Customers
- Vendors/Suppliers
- Independent contractors
- Government
- The Public

For a project for your business, stakeholders can be:

- You
- Your managers (that work for you)
- Your employees
- Your competitors
- Your clients/customers
- Vendors/suppliers
- Independent contractors
- Government
- The public

You can start with the lists above and create a list of your project's stakeholders. Update the list as you go. It will help you create clarity.

Case Studies – List of Stakeholders

Fence Project – Stakeholder List

List of Stakeholders Roles and Names:

(for privacy reasons, some names will not be included in this book)

Stakeholder Role	Stakeholder Name
Project sponsor	Orit
Project manager	David
Material delivery	Home Depot delivery person
Material delivery	Lowes delivery person
Post digging expert	David
Post setting expert	David
Fence Assembly expert	David
Site cleanup specialist	David
Feedback provider	Orit, our four daughters

SCD for Life Project – Stakeholder List

List of Stakeholder Roles and Names

(for privacy reasons, some names will not be included in this book)

Stakeholder Role	Stakeholder Name
Project sponsor	Orit
Project manager	Orit
Online shopper	David
Ingredients chopper	David
Cook	Orit
Curious observers	Our four kids
Update seekers	The grandparents
Author of SCD book	A medical doctor that believes and promotes SCD, based in Seattle
SCD consultant	coordinator of the SCD group on Facebook
SCD advisers	The mothers that are part of the SCD Facebook group
Medical experts	The doctors at UCLA Medical Center, Cedar Sinai Medical Center, and Harvard University/Boston Children's Hospital, and other hospitals that have been involved in our child's care
2nd Opinion Providers	Chron's and Colitis Foundation of America (CCFA) staff, CCFA volunteers
3rd Opinion Providers	The grandparents (grandparents always have opinions!)

More About Your Project's Stakeholders

In larger, more formal projects, you should also include each person's title and contact information (See Figure 5).

Stakeholder Role	Stakeholder Name	Stakeholder Title	Stakeholder Contact Information

Figure 5 - Stakeholder Information

It would be best to classify each stakeholder as either Internal or External (to your organization). Finally, you should specify if you believe they are a **Supporter**, **Resistor,** or **Neutral** about the project. Add these two columns to the previous table (See Figure 6):

Internal / External	Supporter / Resistor / Neutral

Figure 6 - Additional Stakeholder Information

Step 3 – Plan

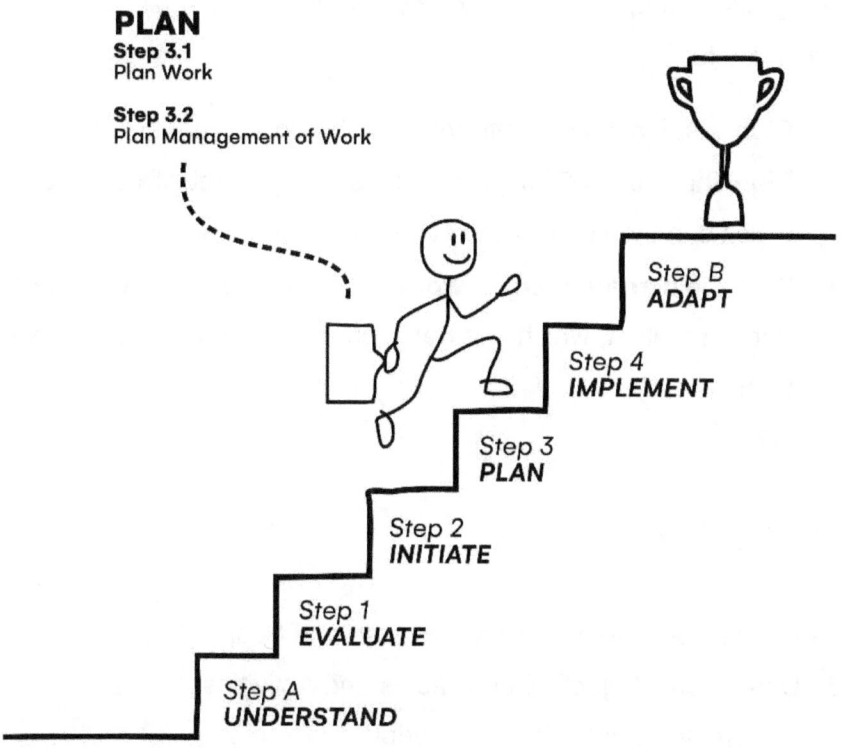

Step 3 - Overview

You will learn to plan projects systematically. Step-by-step. The methodology discussed, once practiced by you again and again in the real world, should allow you to:

- **Plan small projects**, informally, with pen and paper, or in your head
- **Plan the work of larger projects** using a set of documented plans which can then be provided to the project team
- **Plan the management of work** using formal Project Management Plan documentation, which can help you professionally manage the project team

Step 3 - Outline

Step 3.1 - Define Your Project's Requirements and Scope

Step 3.2 - Detail Your Project's Deliverables and Activities

Step 3.3 - Determine Your Project's Schedule

Step 3.4 - Determine Your Project's Human Resource Requirements

Step 3.5 - Determine Your Project's Non-Human Resource Requirements

Step 3.6 - Determine Your Project's Costs and Budget

Step 3.7 - Determine the Risks Involved in Your Project and Responses to Them

Step 3.8 - Define Project Communication

Step 3.9 - Define Project Procurement

Step 3.10 - Define Stakeholder Engagement

Step 3.11 - Define the Quality of Project Deliverables and Activities

Step 3.12 - Plan Change Management

Step 3.13 - Plan Larger and/or More Formal Projects: The Project Management Plan

Step 3 - Objectives

You should be able to create a requirements document for your project

You should be able to create a scope document for your project

You should be able to create a Work Breakdown Structure (WBS) for your project

You should be able to create a Gantt Chart Schedule for your project

You should be able to create an HR plan for your project

You should be able to create a Budget for your project

You should be able to create a Risk Response Plan for your project

You should be able to create a Communication Plan for your project

You should be able to create a Procurement Plan for your project

You should be able to create a Stakeholder Engagement Plan for your project

You should be able to create a Quality Testing Plan for your project

You should be able to create a Change Management Plan for your project

You should be able to create a Project Management Plan for your project

Step 3.1 - Define Your Project's Requirements and Scope

Outline

- Why Break Down the Requirements Further?
- How to Break Down the Requirements Further?
- Define Project Requirements
- Case Studies – Project Requirements
- What is Project Scope?
- Why is Defining Project Scope Important?
- What is Included in a Project Scope Statement?
- Case Studies – Project Scope

Introduction

You and your project made it to the beginning of the planning step of the project! Congratulations!

You will recall that we previously identified the high-level requirements for the Project Charter document. At this stage, we break down the higher-level requirements to their components and possibly sub-components.

Why Break Down the Requirements Further?

To create clarity. The relevant stakeholders need to understand and agree on what the project is required to achieve. Any uncertainties or disagreements about the requirement details should be resolved at this time.

How to Break Down the Requirements Further?

How do you know how far down to go? How many levels of requirements and sub-requirements to have? That depends on the project's complexity and your and your team member's understanding of the requirements.

You break requirements down until you get to a point they are very clear and understood by the relevant team members.

Define Project Requirements

Take the time to interview the relevant stakeholders. Your goal is to determine and document stakeholder needs and requirements to meet the project's objectives. If you are not clear on any of their requirements, ask for clarifications.

The list of requirements should be categorized by stakeholder and priority. These can be documented in a Requirements Document (See Table 1).

Requirement ID	Requirement Description	Stakeholder Proposing Requirement	Priority

Table 1 – List of Requirements

Case Studies – Project Requirements

Fence Project – Stakeholder List

Requirement ID	Requirement Description	Stakeholder Proposing Requirement	Priority
1	The fence must be beautiful	Orit	1
2	The fence should be painted white	Orit	1
3	The fence should completely block the view of the front yard from the street	David	1
4	The fence must be at least 6ft tall, given my height	David	1
5	Dig holes with an auger. Not critical. If the auger is too expensive, I can dig with a shovel	David	3
6	Complete fence in 2-3 weeks would be ideal, but if it takes longer, then be it	David	2
...	...	...	...

SCD for Life Project – Stakeholder List

Requirement ID	Requirement Description	Stakeholder Proposing Requirement	Priority
1	Find a list of foods that everyone that has tried agrees that the food is legal for SCD stage 0.	Orit	1
2	Make sure that the foods proposed for stage 0 are tasty. It would be nice for the child, but not critical if they are not too tasty	Orit	2
3	The chicken must be Kosher since we keep Kosher	David	1
…	…	…	…

What is Project Scope?

Clarifying what you plan to accomplish and what could be but is not included in the project is known as **Project Scope**.

Why is Defining Project Scope Important?

It creates understanding among the project's stakeholders and reduces the opportunity for conflicts during the project and once the project is completed.

It would be impossible to properly plan the other aspects of the project unless you have a clear understanding and agreement among relevant stakeholders on what is required as part of your project.

What is Included in a Project Scope Statement?

A good scope statement includes the following components:

- Description of Product, Service, or DIK that will be created as an outcome of the project.
- **Scope** – what will be done as part of the project?
- **Assumptions** – what assumptions are made about or related to the project?
- **Constraints** – What issues limit what your project is trying to accomplish?
- **Out of Scope** – what is not included as part of the project?
- **Deliverables** – what will be delivered during and or at the conclusion of your project? (present high-level deliverables only at this stage. Once the scope statement is defined, you will proceed to the next stage, where you will discuss the deliverables in greater detail)

- **Acceptance Criteria** – what will constitute a successful conclusion of the project?

Case Studies – Project Scope

Fence Project - Scope

Scope description: 6-foot-high wooden fence, 200 feet in length, with 4x4 posts set in 2 ft deep concrete. The pickets are all on one side of the rails with no gaps (See Figure 14 in Appendix A)

Scope description:
- The project will include the construction of a fence.

Assumptions:
- No rainy days to cause project delays as it is late spring here in Southern California.

Constraints:
- A 30 ft high tree with spreading roots near the path of the fence.
- Bushes along the 200 ft frontage of the house with some roots may make digging the holes more time-consuming.

Out of scope:

- Irrigation – there currently is no irrigation system, and none will be installed as part of this project.
- New landscaping – the existing landscaping will remain in place.
- Gate(s) – the existing front gate, as well as garage gate, will remain in place.

Deliverables:
- 26 holes that are 2 ft deep and 6 inches wide
- 26 posts set in concrete
- Three horizontal rails installed between each pair of adjacent posts
- 320 pickets attached to rails

Acceptance criteria:
- Pickets all installed at the same height
- No gaps between pickets
- And of course, a wife that is happy with the project

SCD for Life Project - Scope

Product description: Stool free of blood

Scope description:
Evaluate the SCD diet to determine if it helps reduce or completely eliminate the symptoms of our daughter's Crohn's.

Assumptions:

Western medicine pushes drugs and operations, while for the most part ignoring that some diseases may be treated in natural ways.

Constraints:

Our daughter was actively bleeding and losing weight again now that we stopped the medications to test this diet. The testing cannot go on for an extended period if we do not start seeing positive results quickly (eliminated or at least reduced blood in the stool).

Out of scope
- Continuing with the drugs, she started taking while at UCLA medical center
- Chinese medicine (herbs and acupuncture) - we tried previously, and it did not work for her
- Vegan diet – we tried previously as well, and it did not work for her

Deliverables
- Stage 0 food to start with
- Stool with no blood (or less blood than when we started with the diet)

Deliverables for Future Project Phases (outside the scope of this initial phase and outside the scope of this book):
- Create and provide stage 1 foods
- If no new bleeding for 3-4 months, create and provide stage 2 foods
- If no new bleeding for 3-4 months, create and provide stage 3 foods
- If no new bleeding for 3-4 months, create and provide stage 4 foods
- If no new bleeding for 3-4 months, create and provide stage 5 foods

Acceptance criteria:
- No blood in the stool (or less blood)
- No weight loss during the three-day period on SCD stage 0
- No abdominal area pains

Step 3.2 - Detail Your Project's Deliverables and Activities

Outline

Why Break Down Your Projects into Parts?
What is a Deliverable?
What is an Activity?
Rules for Breaking Down Deliverables or Activities Further
The WBS Hierarchy
WBS with Deliverables and Sub-Deliverables
WBS with Deliverables, Sub-Deliverables, Activities, and Sub-Activities
Draw a Diagram of Your Project's WBS
A Top-Down Approach to Creating Your WBS
A Bottom-Up Approach to Creating Your WBS
Case Studies – WBS with Deliverables and Sub-Deliverables Only (Chart Format)
Case Studies – WBS with Deliverables, Sub-Deliverables, Activities, Sub-Activities (List Format)
Case Studies – WBS with Deliverables, Sub-Deliverables, Activities, Sub-Activities (Chart Format)

Why Break Down Your Projects into Parts?

You want to achieve your goal. This is why you are working on your project. The project may seem overwhelming, but it does not have to be. The way to deal with what appears to be a complex situation is to break it down into its parts. Each part should be small enough so that you and others involved in the project will be able to understand it. Sometimes this means breaking it down again and again into smaller and smaller parts. When all parts and sub-parts of the project are clear, you will put them all together.

Two basic rules:

- There should be no gaps between project parts
- There should not be an overlap between project parts

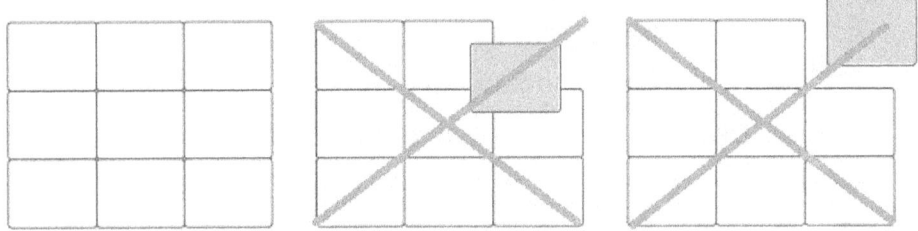

Determining the parts and sub-parts may take a bit of effort on your part.

Different people, organizations, and software applications that help with the management of projects call these parts by different names:

- Components
- Deliverables
- Work Packages
- Activities
- Tasks

In this book, we will look at breaking down a project first to Deliverables (and Sub-Deliverables if and where needed) and then to Activities (and Sub-Activities if and where required).

What is a Deliverable?

A **Deliverable** is a good, service, or DIK that is an (expected) outcome of a project.

What is an Activity?

An **Activity** is one or more actions to accomplish work, leading to completing a project's deliverable(s).

Rules for Breaking Down Deliverables or Activities Further

There are three situations when you should break down a deliverable into two or more sub-deliverables (or a task to two or more sub-tasks):

- When two or more intermediate deliverables (or activities) are needed to produce a final deliverable (or activities)
- When you are unable to estimate the activities accurately, you need to perform work to produce this deliverable (or task), that is, if you are

unable to estimate any of the following to complete the deliverable (or accomplish an activity):
- Human resources
- Non-Human Resources:
    - Equipment
    - Materials
- Financial Resources (costs)
- Facilities
- DIK
- Time to complete

- When the person who will have to do the work is not likely to clearly understand what needs to be done (this person can be you).

The WBS Hierarchy

The following diagram (see Figure 7) shows the hierarchy I recommend for WBS diagrams. It first breaks down projects into deliverables and, if needed, their sub deliverables (there can be more than two levels of deliverables), and then to activities and sub-activities required to create the deliverables (there can be more than two levels of activities).

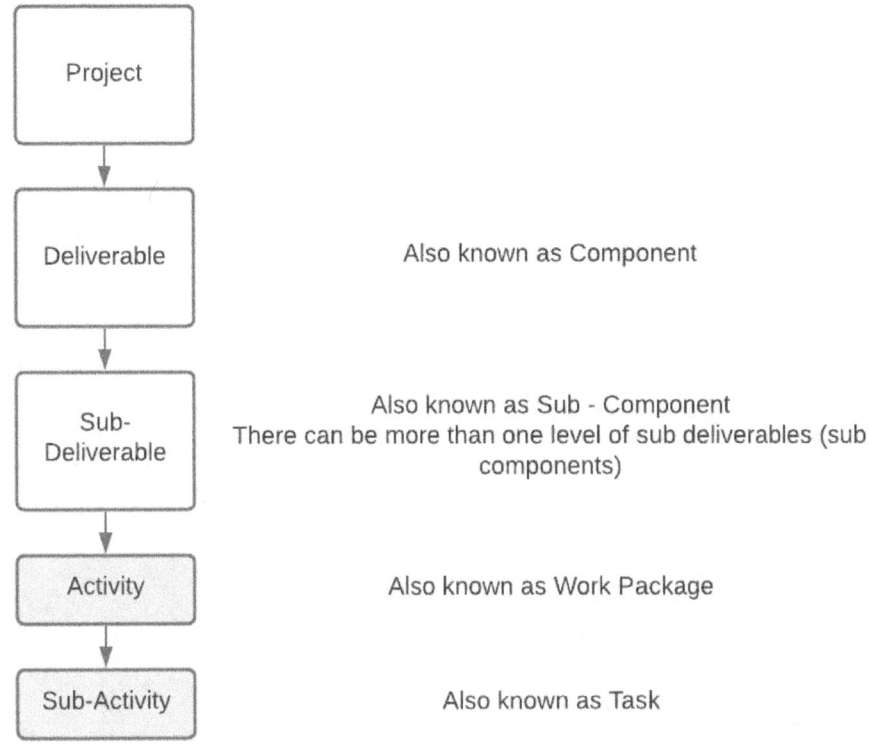

Figure 7 - WBS Hierarchy Explained

WBS with Deliverables and Sub-Deliverables

The following diagram (see Figure 8) is a partial example of a project with multiple deliverables and sub deliverables. Note that a real-world project may require a large diagram that spans many pages.

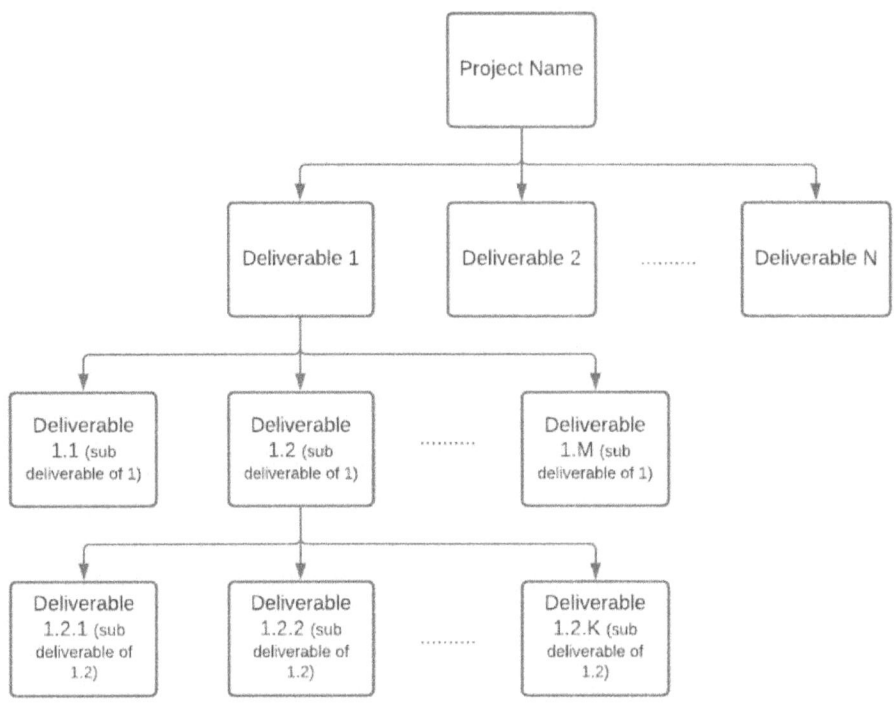

Figure 8 – Sample WBS - Deliverables and Sub-Deliverables Only

WBS with Deliverables, Sub-Deliverables, Activities, and Sub-Activities

The following diagram (see Figure 9) builds on the previous diagram. It is a partial example of a project with multiple deliverables and sub deliverables and activities and sub-activities. Note that a real-world project may require a large diagram that spans many pages.

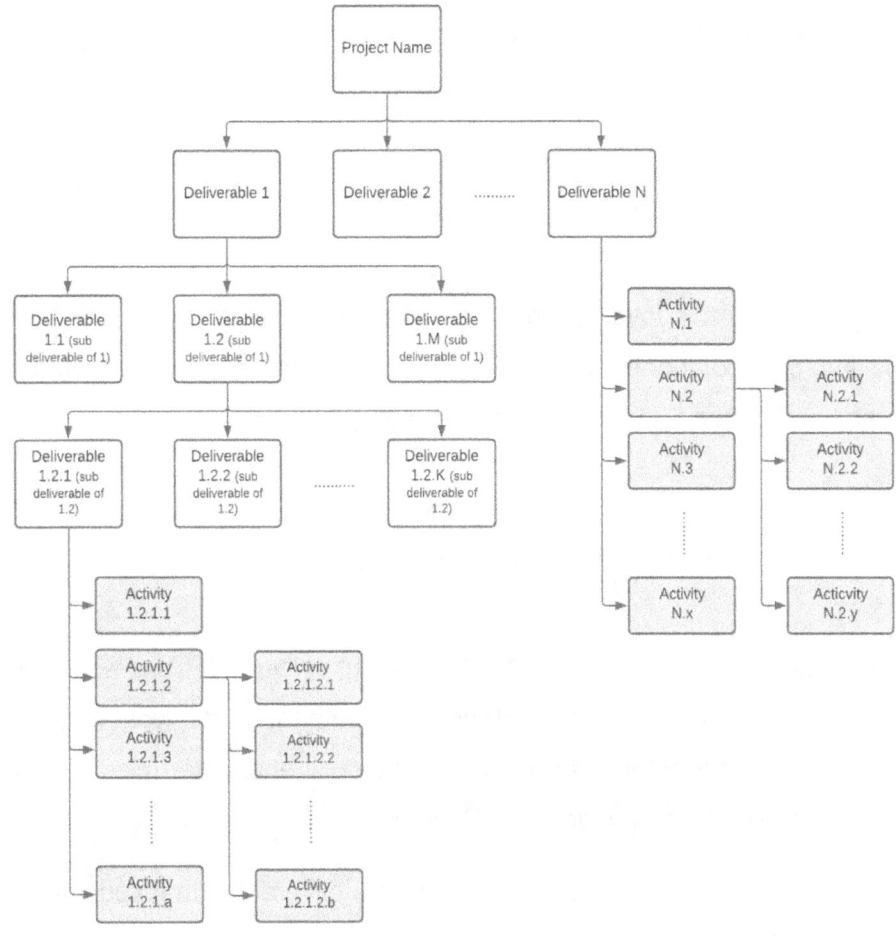

Figure 9 - WBS Sample - Deliverables, Sub-Deliverables, Activities, and Sub-Activities

Draw a Diagram of Your Project's WBS

Draw a diagram of these components (you can draw it online if this is a formal project) or do so with a pen and paper if you are working on a personal/informal project.

There are multiple applications for drawing charts that are available online.

You can create the WBS for your project in one of two ways: top-down or bottom-up.

A Top-Down Approach to Creating Your WBS

Start at the top level of the hierarchy and systematically break WBS elements into their component parts. This approach is more appropriate when you have a reasonably good understanding of the project.

A Bottom-Up Approach to Creating Your WBS

Brainstorm to generate different ideas about deliverables and activities that would be part of your project. Once you come up with the parts, work to figure out how to put them all together. As you do this, you will encounter missing parts of the project and send them into your WBS as well.

Basically, identify intermediate and final deliverables that you think your project will produce and then group them together into larger categories with common characteristics that create the higher levels of the WBS.

Once done creating the draft WBS with the bottom-up approach, you can use the top-down approach to refine it further.

Case Studies – WBS with Deliverables and Sub-Deliverables Only (Chart Format)

The following are the deliverables and sub-deliverables in WBS format for the two case studies we are following in this book:

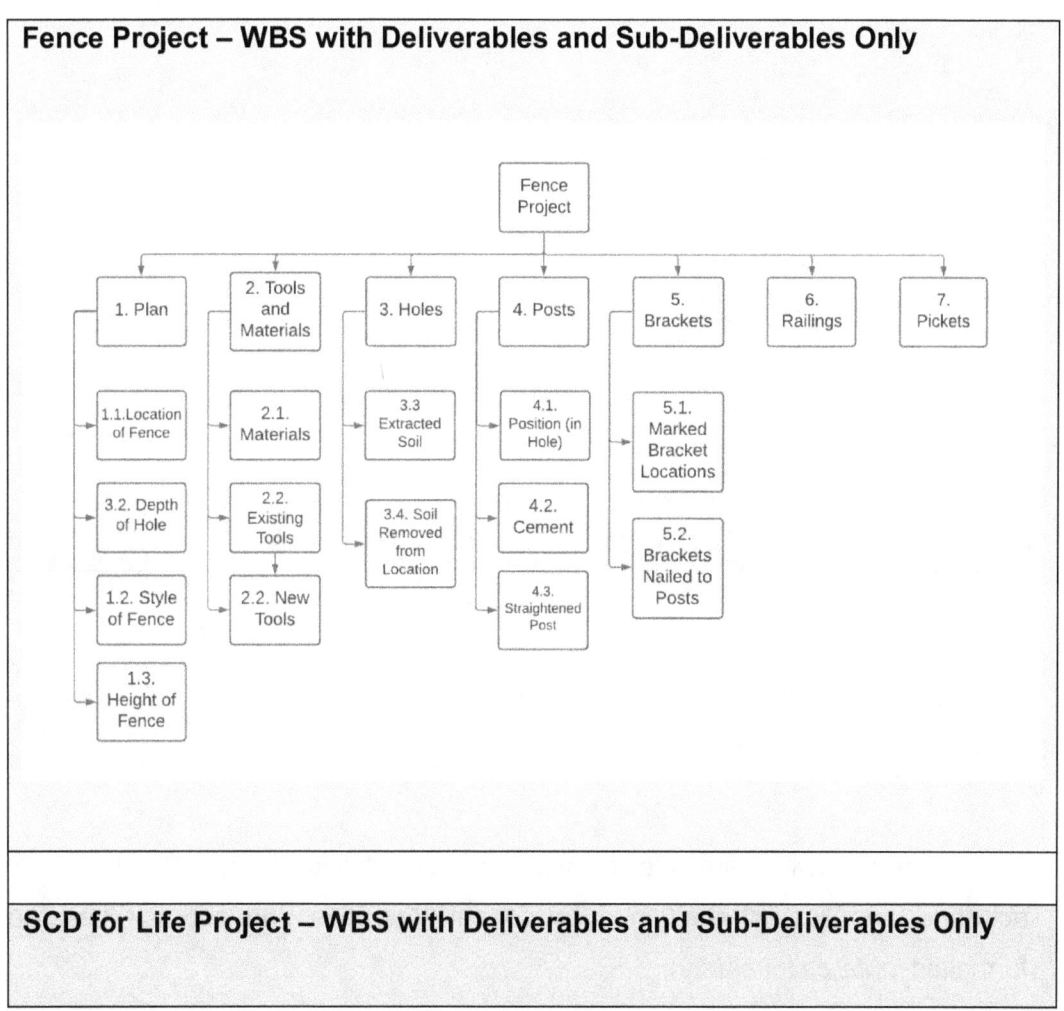

Fence Project – WBS with Deliverables and Sub-Deliverables Only

SCD for Life Project – WBS with Deliverables and Sub-Deliverables Only

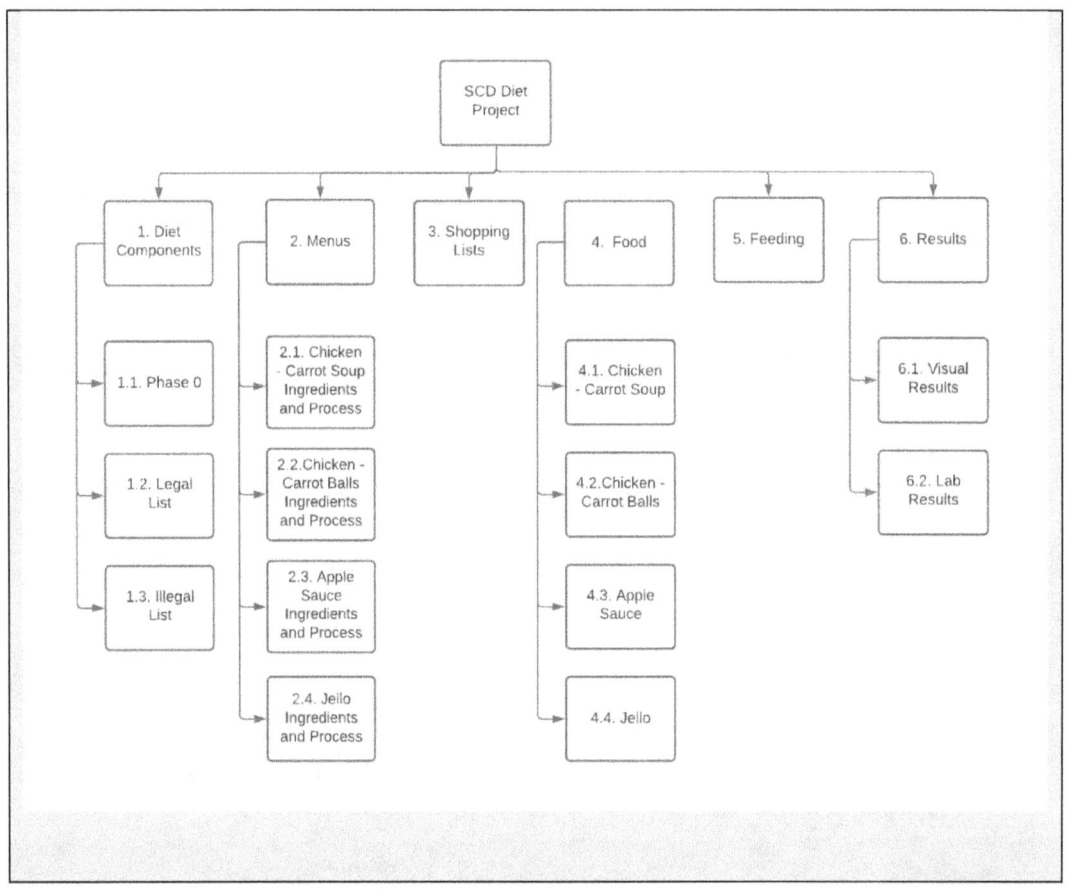

Case Studies – WBS with Deliverables, Sub-Deliverables, Activities, Sub-Activities (List Format)

The following are the deliverables, sub-deliverables, AS WELL AS activities, and sub-activities in a list format (Activities and sub-activities are formatted in *italics* for clarity).

Note that it may take you multiple iterations to get to this level of detail on your own projects. This is normal. You cannot be expected to come up with all the details of your project at one time.

For more complex projects, it is suggested to create an initial list, print it, then when you are "in the zone", come back to it and redline it, then go back to the computer and update the document.

Note how the Activities and Sub-Activities all start with a verb.

Fence Project – WBS with Deliverables, Sub-Deliverables, Activities, Sub-Activities (List Format)

1. Plan of a Fence
    1.1. Location of fence
        1.1.1. Define hole locations - Mark the location of all holes before digging to make sure the fence ends up being installed in a straight line
            1.1.1.1. Mark the center of the first hole with spray paint
            1.1.1.2. Mark the center of the last hole with spray paint
            1.1.1.3. Place a second stake in the ground
            1.1.1.4. Tie a rope to the first stake
            1.1.1.5. Stretch the rope all the way to the second stake
            1.1.1.6. Tie the rope around the second stake such that the rope is tight in the air 3-4 inches above the ground
            1.1.1.7. Mark location of posts on the ground every 8 ft along the rope
    1.2. Depth of holes
        1.2.1. Determine the depth of holes (internet research)

1.3. Style of fence
- 1.3.1. *Look at different options (internet research) and select style (See* Figure 15 *for the fence style selected)*
1.4. Height of fence
- 1.4.1. *Determine at the max allowed in the area (walk the neighborhood and internet research)*

2. Tools and Materials
   2.1. Materials
   - 2.1.1. *Define what materials are needed for the project*
   - 2.1.2. *Calculate how many items are needed from each materials category*
   - 2.1.3. *Compare prices and order materials*
     - 2.1.3.1. *Visit HomeDepot.com and/or Lowes.com, compare prices*
     - 2.1.3.2. *Order posts*
     - 2.1.3.3. *Order rails*
     - 2.1.3.4. *Order pickets*
     - 2.1.3.5. *Order brackets*
     - 2.1.3.6. *Order nails*
     - 2.1.3.7. *Order fast setting concrete mix for posts*
   - 2.1.4. *Receive deliveries*
     - 2.1.4.1. *Request each delivery package or crate be placed in front of the main gate and not the garage gate to minimize the distance between the delivery site and locations where materials will be placed inside the front yard*
     - 2.1.4.2. *Count which items received in each delivery and how many, and record against what was ordered*

- 2.1.5. Move delivered tools and materials from street to front yard
    - 2.1.5.1. Identify three locations in the front yard along the 200 ft frontage and place one-third of the materials in each location (every 50 ft).
- 2.2. Existing Tools
    - 2.2.1. Find existing tools and equipment, and bring them to the front yard
        - 2.2.1.1. Find my Level in the garage
        - 2.2.1.2. Find hammer in the garage
        - 2.2.1.3. Find Tape Measure in the garage. If not found, order a new one
        - 2.2.1.4. Find two 5-gallon buckets in back yard farm
        - 2.2.1.5. Find a rake in the farm
        - 2.2.1.6. Find a shovel in the farm
- 2.3. New Tools
    - 2.3.1. Order an auger - a gas-powered tool to dig holes – compare prices at HomeDepot, Lowes, Amazon
    - 2.3.2. Order any tools/equipment that was not found
    - 2.3.3. Make sure all tools/equipment received

Auger:

    2.3.4. Assemble and test the auger
        2.3.4.1. Watch one or more YouTube videos to learn how to assemble and operate the auger
        2.3.4.2. Read the manual that came with the auger
        2.3.4.3. Find two wrenches
        2.3.4.4. Follow instructions to connect the two parts of the auger with a bolt
        2.3.4.5. Mix gas with engine oil and fill in the auger's tank
        2.3.4.6. Start the engine
3. Holes
    3.1. Extracting soil
        3.1.1. Drill hole and extract soil using an auger
            3.1.1.1. Place the auger centered about the mark for each hole
            3.1.1.2. Turn on the engine per instructions. The auger bit starts spinning

3.1.1.3. Push the auger towards the soil
3.1.1.4. Press on the Throttle
3.1.1.5. The auger bit will start removing the soil.
3.1.1.6. Keep going until you reach a point when the auger is not able to go any deeper.
3.1.1.7. Turn off the auger
3.1.1.8. Remove the soil from the hole
3.1.1.9. If a hole is not yet two feet deep, turn the auger again and proceed as above.

3.2. Moving soil away from the site
    3.2.1. Move soil away from the site
        3.2.1.1. Fill extracted soil into a bucket
        3.2.1.2. Take the bucket to off worksite location and empty it

4. Posts
    4.1. Position (in a hole)
        4.1.1. Bring the post from the nearest pile and place a post inside a hole
    4.2. Cement
        4.2.1. Pour Cement in Hole
            4.2.1.1. Bring a bag of concrete mix and place it in front of the hole
            4.2.1.2. Cut the bag open with a knife
            4.2.1.3. Hold the post straight such that it is centered inside the hole with one hand, and push the content of the open concrete mix bag into the hole.
            4.2.1.4. Place the level against the post to make sure it is standing straight. Adjust the post as needed.

4.3. Straightened post
- 4.3.1. Straighten the post using water and a level.
    - 4.3.1.1. *Once the post is in position, place the end of the water hose inside the hole and turn the water on. Make sure the water fills in the hole all the way, and then turn off the water (the water will combine with the dry concrete mix and solidify quickly).*
    - 4.3.1.2. *Use the level against the post to make sure it is still standing straight. Adjust the post if needed.*
    - 4.3.1.3. *Come back to the post in 10 minutes and add more water. More water translates to stronger concrete.*
    - 4.3.1.4. *Come back to the posts you installed that day just before you are done with work for the day, and add more water to all of them.*

Bracket:

5. Brackets
    - 5.1. Marked Bracket Locations
        - 5.1.1. Mark bracket locations
            - 5.1.1.1. *Mark position of lower bracket one foot from the ground (see picture above)*
            - 5.1.1.2. *mark middle bracket two feet above the lower bracket*

5.1.1.3. mark the upper bracket two feet above the middle bracket

5.2. Brackets Nailed to Posts

5.2.1. Nail brackets to posts

5.2.1.1. Install lower bracket one foot from the ground (see picture above)

5.2.1.2. Install middle bracket two feet above the lower bracket

5.2.1.3. Install the upper bracket two feet above the middle bracket

Railing (horizontal):

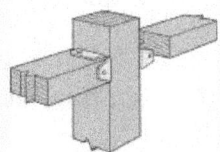

6. Railings

6.1. Install Rails between posts

6.1.1. Install lower rail one foot from the ground

6.1.2. Install middle rail two feet above the lower rail

6.1.3. Install the upper rail two feet above the middle rail

6.1.4. Hammer three nails into each bracket connecting it to the wood rail inside it.

7. Pickets

7.1. Attach pickets to rails

7.1.1. Take a nail and a hammer in one hand

7.1.2. Take the picket in the other hand

7.1.3. Line up the bottom of the picket you are about to install with the picket previously installed next to it, such that there is no gap between the pickets.
7.1.4. Hold the picket in place with one hand
7.1.5. Hammer the nail such that it connects the picket to the upper rail.
7.1.6. Make sure the two rails are lined up with no gaps.
7.1.7. Get five more nails
7.1.8. Hammer the second nail such that it connects the picket to the bottom rail
7.1.9. Now that the picket is fixed to the rails, hammer the four remaining nails
    7.1.9.1. Hammer two nails connecting the picket to the middle rail
    7.1.9.2. Hammer a second nail connecting the picket to the upper rail
    7.1.9.3. Hammer a second nail connecting the picket to the lower rail

SCD for Life Project - WBS with Deliverables, Sub-Deliverables, Activities, Sub-Activities (List Format)

1. Diet components
   1.1. Phases
      1.1.1. Research SCD Phase 0
         1.1.1.1. Read about phase 0 on different online web pages

- 1.1.1.2. Learn what is common to the various phase 0 approaches
- 1.1.1.3. Learn what is different
- 1.1.1.4. Ask the authors questions about their perspectives
- 1.1.2. Inform husband about SCD Phase 0
- 1.2. Legal list
- 1.2.1. Create a list of legal foods/ingredients for phase 0 of SCD
- 1.2.2. Print the list and tape to the kitchen cabinet for easy reference
- 1.3. Illegal list
- 1.3.1. Create a list of illegal foods/ingredients for phase 0 of SCD
- 1.3.2. Print the list and tape to the kitchen cabinet for easy reference

2. Menus
- 2.1. Chicken-Carrot Soup Ingredients and Process
- 2.1.1. Research and record chicken-carrot soup ingredients and cooking process
  - 2.1.1.1. Find the largest pot we can find (should be in the garage)
  - 2.1.1.2. Fill in pot 50% with water
  - 2.1.1.3. Place a pot with water on the stove, and turn on the heat
  - 2.1.1.4. Peel 20 carrots, wash, and place in pot
  - 2.1.1.5. Open two packaged whole chickens, wash, and place in pot
  - 2.1.1.6. Let it all come to a boil
  - 2.1.1.7. Reduce the heat to low, cover the pot and let it cook for another 3.5 hours
  - 2.1.1.8. Remove from stove

2.2. Chicken-Carrot Balls Ingredients and Process
- 2.2.1. Research and record chicken-carrot balls ingredients and cooking process
  - 2.2.1.1. Take chicken out of soup
  - 2.2.1.2. Take carrots out of soup
  - 2.2.1.3. Remove chicken bones and skin and dispose
  - 2.2.1.4. Cut chicken into smaller pieces
  - 2.2.1.5. Place chicken pieces and carrots in a food processor and add two raw eggs
  - 2.2.1.6. Blend all three ingredients
  - 2.2.1.7. Place prep gloves on your hands
  - 2.2.1.8. Make chicken-carrot-egg balls
  - 2.2.1.9. Place them back in the soup
  - 2.2.1.10. Let soup cook for another 10 minutes

2.3. Apple Sauce Ingredients and Process
- 2.3.1. Research and record apple sauce ingredients and cooking process
  - 2.3.1.1. Remove apple peel
  - 2.3.1.2. Cook apples
  - 2.3.1.3. Blend apples in a food processor

2.4. Jello Ingredients and Process
- 2.4.1. Research and record jello ingredients and cooking process
  - 2.4.1.1. Place 1/4 cold water in a 1-quart bowl
  - 2.4.1.2. sprinkle the envelope of plain fish or beef gelatin (1 Tablespoon) on top and let it soften.

- 2.4.1.3. *Stir in 3/4 cup of boiling water and honey "to taste" (It might not need any.)*
- 2.4.1.4. *Stir to mix well. Add one cup of fruit juice and stir again.*
- 2.4.1.5. *If you want to put it in a mold, oil the mold and pour in your jello mixture.*
- 2.4.1.6. *Chill until set. This makes six servings.*
3. Shopping Lists
    - 3.1. *Create a shopping list of foods/ingredients to purchase*
    - 3.2. *Purchase ingredients*
4. Food
    - 4.1. Chicken-Carrot Soup
        - 4.1.1. *Prepare chicken-carrot soup*
    - 4.2. Chicken-Carrot Balls
        - 4.2.1. *Prepare chicken-carrot balls*
    - 4.3. Apple Sauce
        - 4.3.1. *Prepare apple sauce*
    - 4.4. Jello
        - 4.4.1. *Prepare jello*
5. Feeding
    - 5.1. *Feed baby (3 days)*
6. Results
    - 6.1. Visual
        - 6.1.1. *Inspect stool*
    - 6.2. Lab results
        - 6.2.1. *Collect stool*
        - 6.2.2. *Visit lab*

> 6.2.3. Hand in stool
> 6.2.4. Test blood
> 6.2.5. Receive results

Case Studies – WBS with Deliverables, Sub-Deliverables, Activities, Sub-Activities (Chart Format)

Below you will find the WBS diagrams of both projects enhanced to include (some of) the Activities and Sub-Activities.

Notice that when you run out of space on your page, one option (but not the only one) is to redirect the flow to another WBS diagram using a shape such as this one (Figure 10).

Figure 10 - Symbol Used to Redirect to Another Diagram

Fence Project - WBS with Deliverables, Sub-Deliverables, Activities, Sub-Activities (Chart Format)

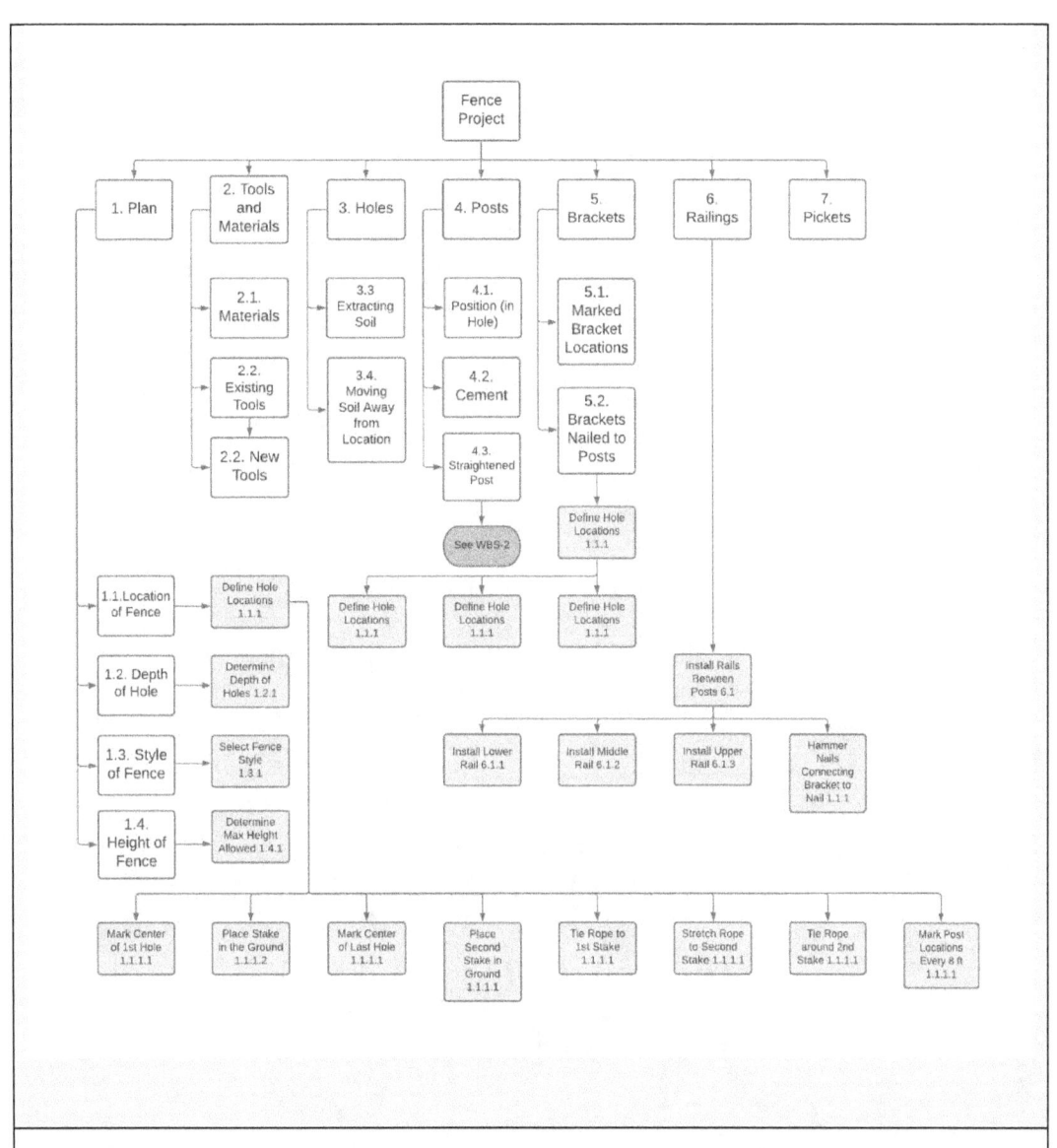

SCD for Life Project - WBS with Deliverables, Sub-Deliverables, Activities, Sub-Activities (Chart Format)

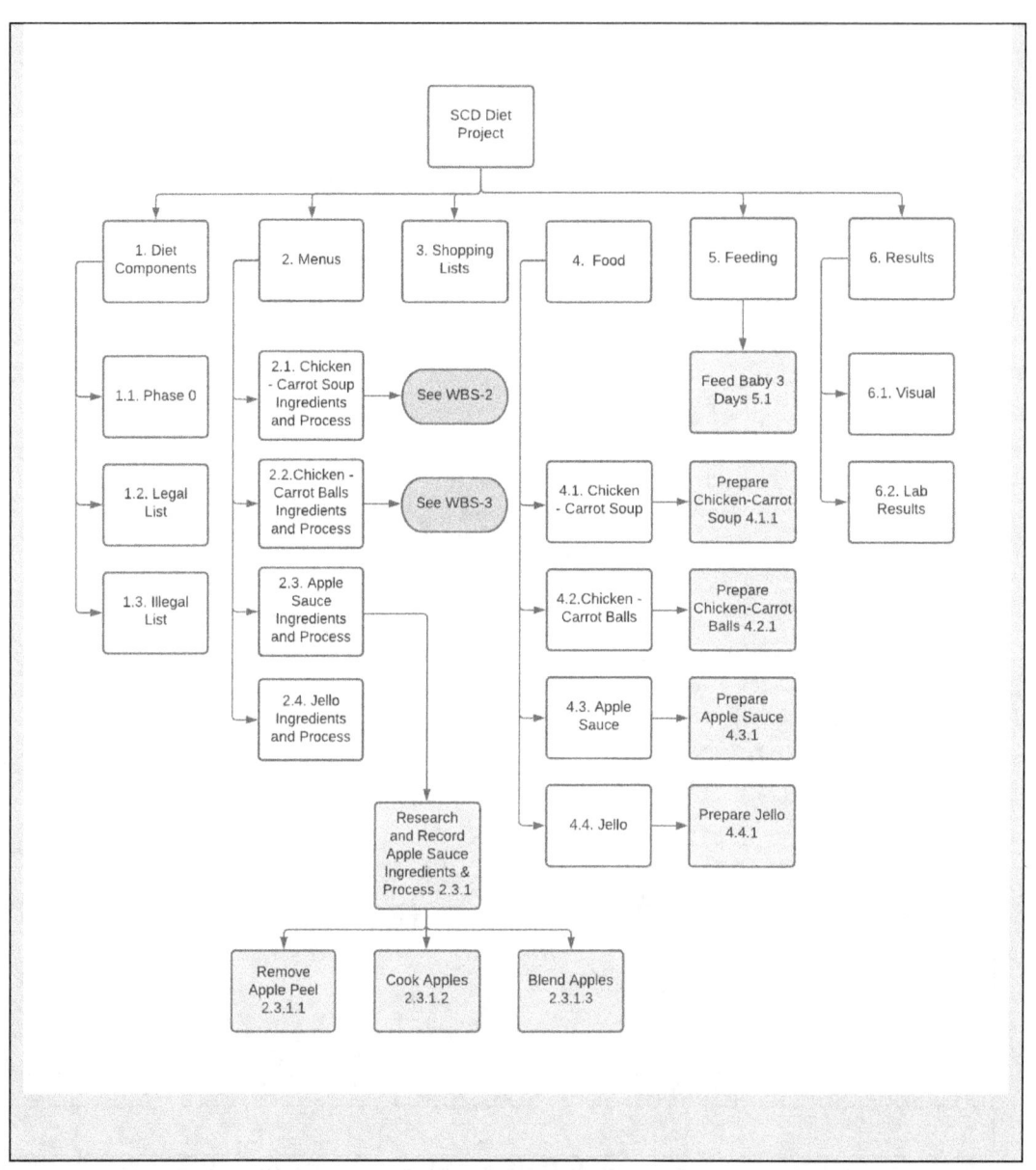

Step 3.3 - Determine Your Project's Schedule

Outline

> What is a Milestone?
> What is Activity Duration?
> Estimate Activity Duration
> Draw a Network Diagram
> Case Studies – Network Diagram
> Identify the Critical Path (Shortest Path)
> Case Studies – Shortest Path Network Diagram
> Project Schedule
> Case Studies - Project Schedule

Introduction

Now that we have defined the deliverables and the activities to create the deliverables, we will determine how much time it will take to complete the project. To achieve this, we will look at network diagrams. **Network Diagrams** consist of activities and their duration. Arrows show the relationships between activities. They may also consist of milestones. Since we are already familiar with Activities, let's jump to discuss the milestones.

What is a Milestone?

A **Milestone** is a moment in time. It is a moment of importance to the project. Itself it takes no time and consumes no resources.

Imagine driving a car from Los Angeles to San Francisco on the 101 freeway. As you drive North, three or so hours into it, you see a sign indicating that beautiful San Luis Obispo is just ahead. In no time, you pass the sign and keep driving. That sign is your milestone.

As a side note, if you ever get a chance to take that trip, stop and visit that beautiful town.

What is Activity Duration?

Activity Duration is the total number of work periods required to complete an activity. It is different from the Work Effort itself, which is the amount of time it takes to do the work.

For example, it may take three and a half hours to get from Los Angeles to San Luis Obispo, thus activity duration of 3.5 hours. The work effort, in this case, would only be 3 hours if 30 minutes were allocated for a rest stop at the Santa Barbara Pier.

Estimate Activity Duration

To estimate activity duration as accurately as possible, you should do the following:

- Use your experience if you have done something similar before

- Use other people's experiences if they have done something similar before (ask them questions)
- Research
- Experiment
- Combine some or all of the above

Realize that some physical processes take time. For example, if you jump into the lake with your clothing, it will take some time for them to dry before you can put them back on.

There may be time delays during which no activity takes place – consider getting a flat tire. You will need to call AAA, and while the technician could replace the tire within 10 minutes, it may take them another 40 minutes to get to you, 5 minutes to complete paperwork and verify your identity, proceed to replace the tire, and once done, chat with you for another 10 minutes.

You can refine the estimates for each activity by asking those that will perform the activities to provide their feedback.

You will likely need to refine these estimates further once you and your team start implementing the project's activities and reality sets in.

Draw a Network Diagram

To create a network diagram, draw the activity that needs to be performed as soon as your project starts. Decide which activity or activities can be performed when you finish the first one and draw them. Continue this way until you finish drawing all activities in the project.

Another way to handle this is to start from the final activity and go backward. With this approach, for each activity, you need to identify which activities must be handled before that activity can be handled. You proceed this way repeatedly until you reach the beginning.

As you build your project's network diagram, you will likely find yourself adding activities to deliverables that you missed previously. If that happens, make sure to update the diagrams we discussed previously as well.

You can draw Milestones, just like activities, except you will note that their duration is 0 units.

Case Studies – Network Diagram

Fence Project – Network Diagram

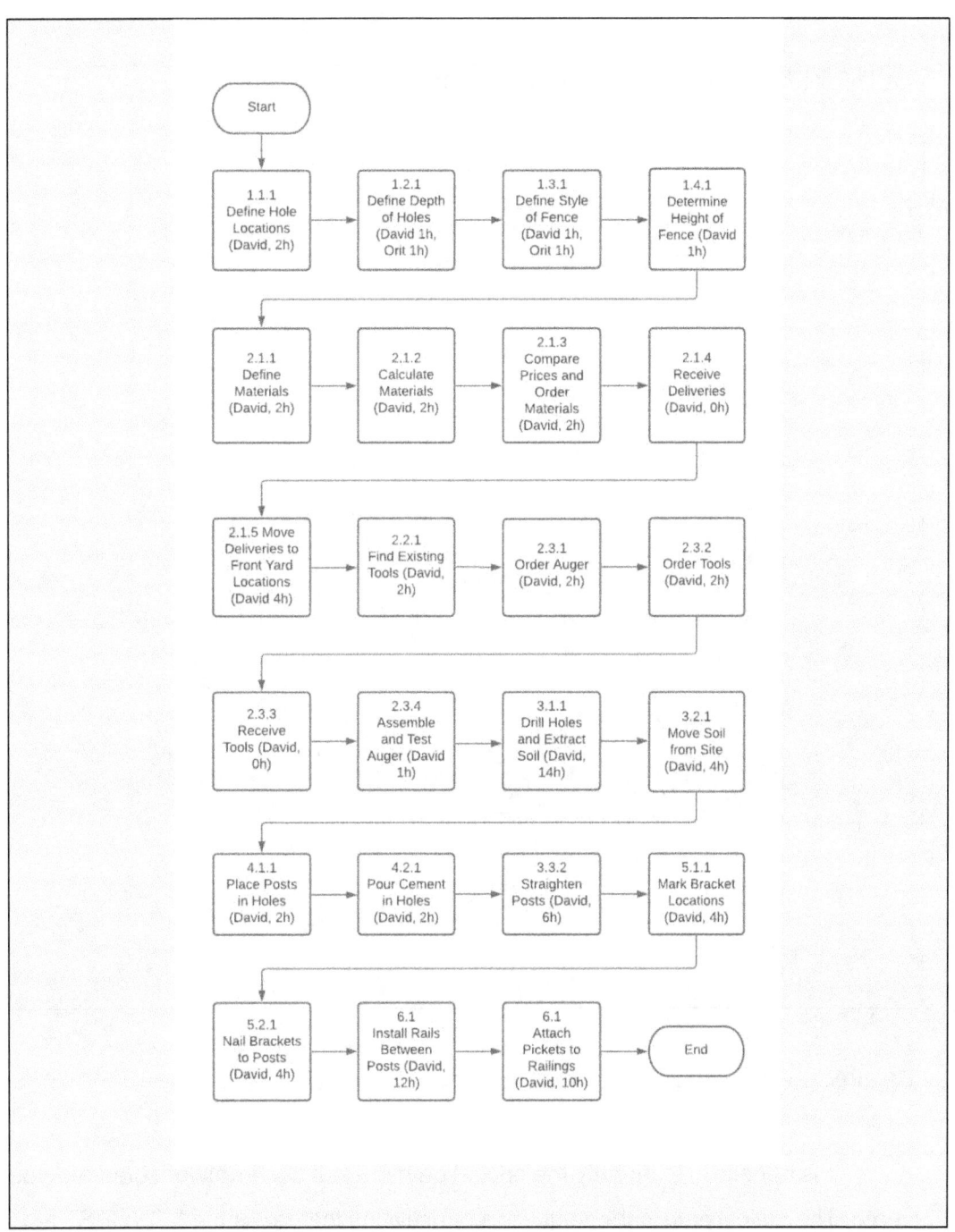

SCD for Life Project – Network Diagram

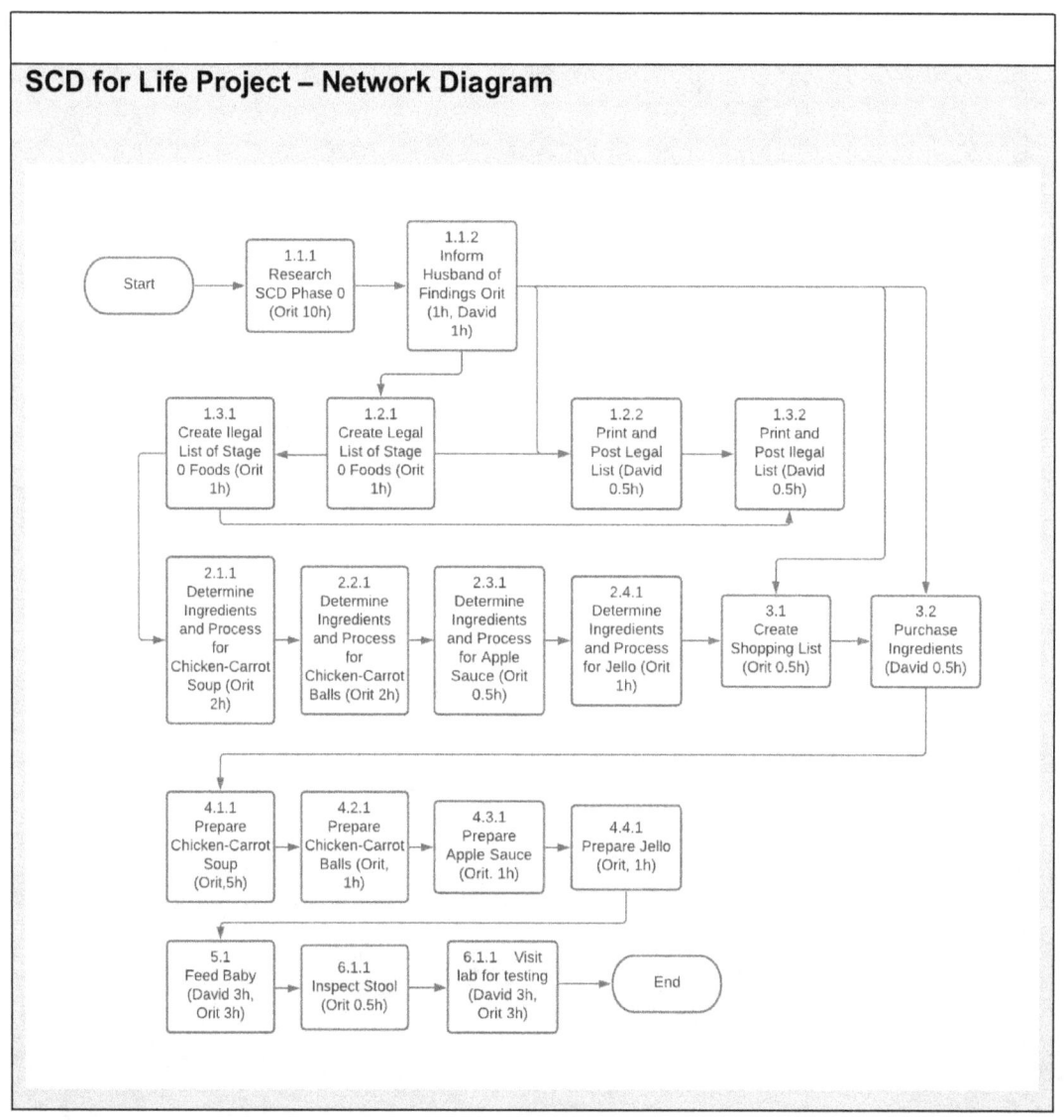

Identify the Critical Path (Shortest Path)

It is beneficial to identify the critical path in each such network diagram you create. The critical path is the sequence of activities that takes the LONGEST time to complete. This is also the SHORTEST time in which you can complete your project.

Why is this concept important? Since if you want to shorten your project's duration, you need to focus on shortening the critical path.

There are two general scenarios for completing projects.

- You have a deadline you must meet.
- You do not have a deadline but wish you complete the project as soon as possible while minimizing costs.

Either way, you should look at your network diagram and then see if you can shorten the critical path by determining if two or more activities can be handled in parallel when your critical path becomes shorter than another path in your diagram. The longer path becomes the critical path. Repeat the process on this new critical path and keep going for all other paths in the network until you can no longer identify ways to shorten the latest critical path. You can also have other people look at your network diagram and see if they can provide their perspective on shortening the critical path.

You can then update your WBS based on your modified Network Diagram.

Case Studies – Shortest Path Network Diagram

Fence Project – Shortest Path Network Diagram

Same as the original network diagram

SCD For Life Project – Shortest Path Network Diagram

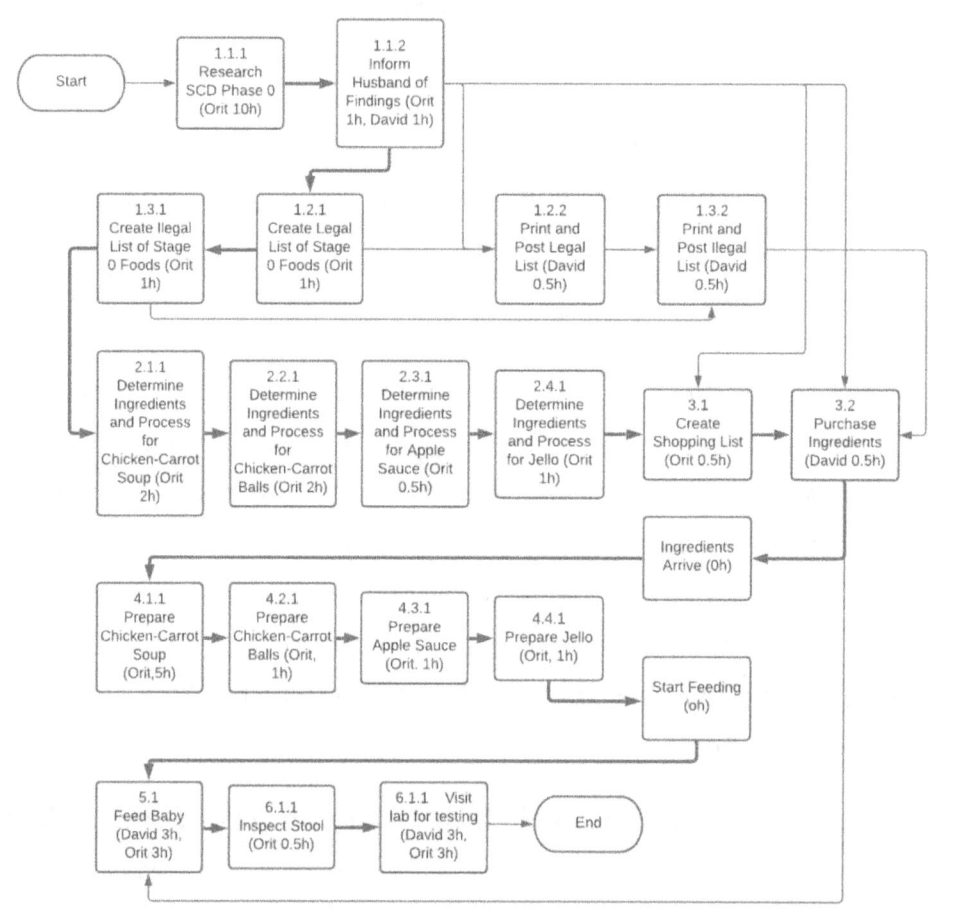

Note that the shortest path is marked with the darker arrows. It takes 17.5 hours to get to the Start Feeding Milestone.

Can this time be shortened? Yes. We can shorten the critical path to get to the Start Feeding milestone by two hours by assigning David to make the apple sauce and jello. See diagram below:

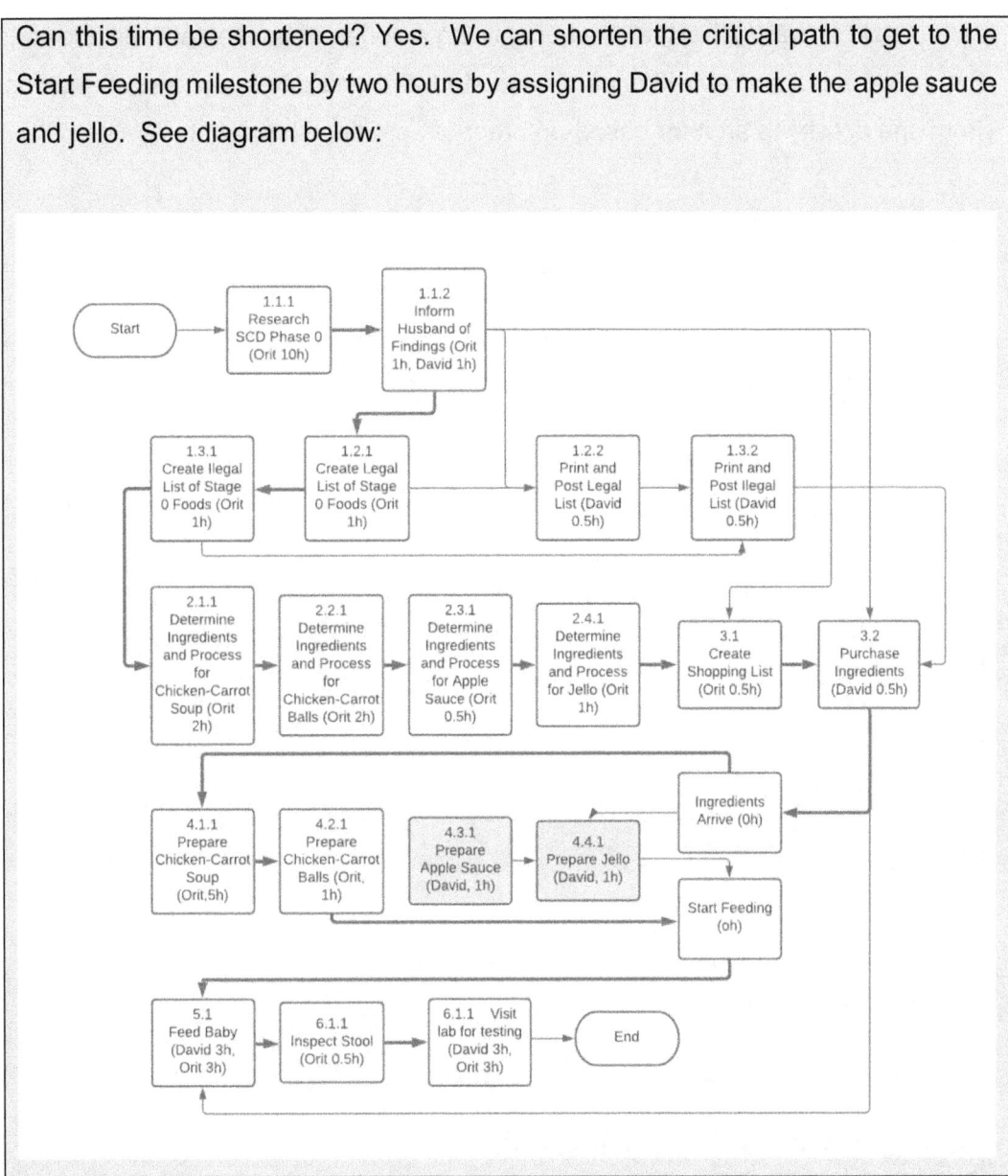

Project Schedule

Add a **Gantt Chart**, a chart containing a series of horizontal lines showing the deliverables and activities as well as start and end dates and arrows leading from one activity to another based-on order of activities shown in the WBS.

Case Studies - Project Schedule

Fence Project – Project Schedule

Fence Project

Plan Duration

ACTIVITY	PLAN START	PLAN DURATION	ACTUAL START	ACTUAL DURATION	PERCENT COMPLETE	PERIODS 1 2 3 4 5 6 7 8
1.1.1 - Define Hole Locations	1	1				
1.2.1 - Define Depth	1	1				
1.3.1 - Define Style	2	1				
1.4.1 - Define Height	2	1				
2.1.1 - Define Materials	3	1				
2.1.2 - Calculate Materials	3	1				
2.1.3 - Compare Prices, Order Materials	4	1				
2.1.4 - Receive Deliverables	7	1				

SCD for Life Project – Project Schedule

SCD for Life Project

ACTIVITY	PLAN START	PLAN DURATION	ACTUAL START	ACTUAL DURATION	PERCENT COMPLETE	PERIODS 1 2 3 4 5 6 7 8
1.1.1 - Research SCD	1	3				
1.1.2 - Inform Husband	3	1				
1.2.1 - Create Legal List	3	1				
1.2.2 - Print Legal List	3	1				
1.3.1 - Create Ilegal List	3	1				
1.3.2 - Print Ilegal List	3	1				
2.2.1 - Determine Ingredients	4	1				

Plan Duration

Step 3.4 - Determine Your Project's Human Resource Requirements

Outline

- What Makes Human Resources Great?
- How to Find Great Human Resources?
- Learn from Others about Your Project
- Assign Human Resources to Activities
- Human Resources for Larger Projects and or Organizations
- Develop a Project Team
- Human Resources Charts for Larger Projects
- Organizational Chart
- Responsibility Matrix
- Role Descriptions

Introduction

You may have already allocated some or all human resources as you worked on the WBS in Step 3.2, and you may think you are done. Still, I encourage you to read the information provided next and see if you need to make any adjustments to your initial assignments.

What Makes Human Resources Great?

Let's first understand two basic definitions that will have a major impact on your project: productivity and efficiency.

Productivity. The results an individual produces for each unit of time that he or she spends on an activity. Typically, one can produce more per unit of time if they are more knowledgeable in the subject matter, have appropriate education and experience, know how to multi-task, and of course, if they have a sense of urgency.

The quality of the physical environment and how it is setup will also have an impact on their productivity.

Efficiency. The share of time an individual spends on an activity instead of other tasks that are not specifically related to it, such as meetings, training, restroom visits, and online shopping.

Ultimately you want to surround yourself with people that are more productive and efficient rather than less.

For each activity, you want people with the relevant skills (the ability to do it well) and experience and, hopefully, motivation. You need to decide what skills and knowledge are needed for each activity.

You should surround yourself with great resources. This is good for your project and your life.

How to Find Great Human Resources?

The process I suggest consists of the following steps (see Figure 11). They are described below.

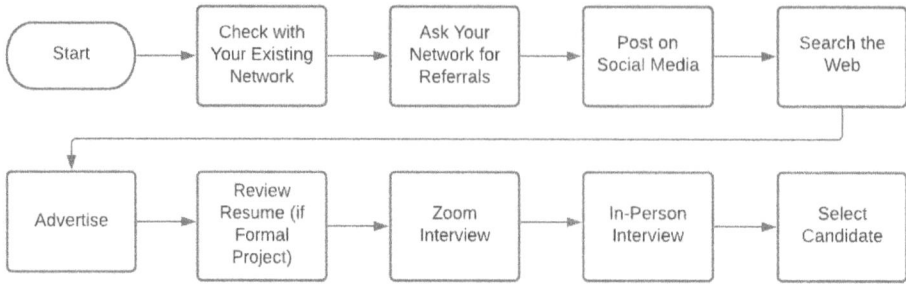

Figure 11 - The Process of Locating and Recruiting Human Resources

Start by looking at your existing personal and professional networks. See if any of them are qualified and interested in joining your project.

The next step is to ask those in your network for referrals to others that might fit your needs (if more candidates are needed). This is a great business networking opportunity, as by asking if people know people, you are indirectly marketing yourself and your business. You can also post messages on your social media asking for recommendations (Facebook or LinkedIn, for example).

The next step is to search the web for specific human resources (if more candidates are needed). There are specific sites that review business professionals in various categories, other websites that may provide recommendations, and yet other websites that facilitate the connection to such professionals.

You might also consider paid advertising for the opportunity in one of the many online job search websites/portals (if more candidates are needed). There are general online job search portals (such as indeed.com and industry-specific job portals in most industries).

It's important not only to focus on "how long" but also on "why" since without the "why", candidates are more likely to underestimate activity durations just to impress you so that they can get the job.

If the project is more formal, you might want to ask for and review candidates' resumes.

The next step is to zoom, zoom, zoom. Speak with candidates, learn about them, their experiences and compare.

Finally, you might consider an in-person interview before making your hiring decisions.

Should you continue to look for more candidates once you find a good candidate? YES, if you have time. Why? You might be able to find a better candidate. Also, you will learn more about your project by talking to more candidates. Finally, it is always good to have backups.

Learn from Others about Your Project

As you go through interviewing various people for a specific position, role in your project, you can ask your candidates how long activities would take and why. This is a great way to determine who is likely to be a better candidate for you but also a way to get some feedback on various aspects of your project at no cost to you (other than your time), as well as find great people to add to your professional network, and possibly to this and/or future projects.

Assign Human Resources to Activities

There is often more than one person that can handle the task and do it well. How long would each candidate take to complete the task? What is their availability? How productive are your resources? How efficient? The more questions you ask, the more you will learn about the individuals you are considering for your project as well as about your actual project.

Ensure your resources are not overloaded. When there is an overload, you can reduce or eliminate it by adjusting the start time of activities, especially where there is slack time (without extending the deadline for the complete project. Sometimes that is not possible, and the project completion date must be extended to accommodate resources and their availability.

Human Resources for Larger Projects and or Organizations

If you work for a company with existing human resources, you may be able to request and or assign existing human resources to your project's activities if they are available and willing to participate.

If you own a business and you have human resources working for you already, you might be able to pull existing human resources into your project (if you believe they could contribute and have time to do so).

Suppose you cannot find appropriate internal resources for your new project, or others are unwilling to pull them from their existing commitments. In that case, you should expand to search for external human resources.

If you work for a larger organization or own one, there may be an HR manager or an HR department that may help you with your project staffing needs.

Develop a Project Team

To maximize the success of larger projects, you might need to work with individual team members and the team as a whole. You should plan as much as possible of what you will need to do once the project starts.

Enhance Individual Performance - Develop individual team members' skills, understand where each person is, where they need to be and how to get them there. Enhancing individual performance could include any of the following:

- Assigning a mentor
- Formal training
- Informal Training
- Rewards for success
- Punishment for lack of success

Enhance Team Performance – Many things can contribute to enhanced team performance. These include enhancing team communications - You should plan to ensure your team members are working effectively and efficiently together to achieve a common goal. We will discuss communication later in Step 3.8

Human Resources Charts for Larger Projects

When a project starts getting larger, with more people on your project team and outside of it, consider drawing diagrams to showcase the situation. Three of the more common diagrams are shown next.

Organizational Chart

An **Organizational Chart** (Org Chart) shows people, roles as well as the relationships between them. See Figure 12 below.

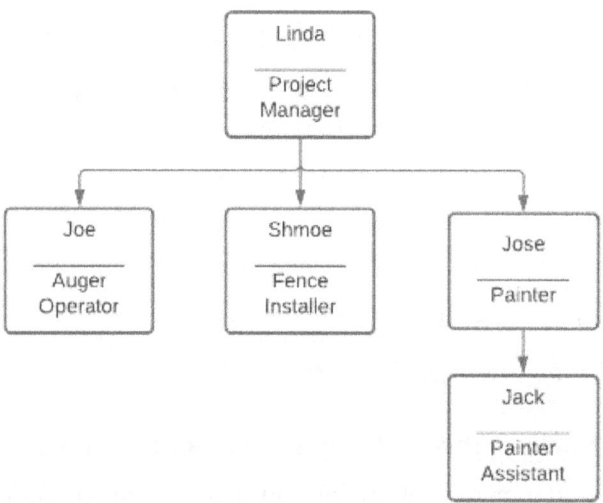

Figure 12 - Organization Chart

Responsibility Matrix

A **Responsibility Matrix** is shown in Table 2 below. It identifies who is responsible for which activity and to what extent.

In the left-most column, you will list all your project activities (the ones from your WBS). On the top, you will list your human resources/team members' names and roles.

There are four categories of responsibilities, denoted as following in the responsibility matrix:

- R – Responsible – the person is responsible for the activity or sub-activity
- A – Accountable – the person is responsible for a portion of the activity but not necessarily for the overall activity.
- C – Consulted – The person is to be consulted on the work related to the activity but is not necessarily accountable for it.
- I – Informed – The person should be kept informed of the progress and/or outcome of the activity.

Activity Name	Project Manager Linda	Team Member Joe	Team Member Shmoe	Team Member Jose	...
Create…	R	A	C	I	
Assemble…	I	R	A	C	

Table 2 - Responsibility Matrix

Role Descriptions

For each role, specify (See Table 3):
- The brief descriptive name of the role
- Description of the role
- Specific Responsibilities
- Authority provided to the person that will assume the role

Role: Cook (at Restaurant)
Description: The cook will be responsible for all aspects of each food order from the time it is received from the server to the time the food is provided to the server to deliver to the customer.
Responsibilities: • Cook the food specified in the order of each customer • Assemble food on the plate per specifications • Place the food order in the pickup area for the servers to pick up and deliver to the customers

Authority:

- Authorized to delegate work to three assistant cooks
- Authorized to prioritize incoming orders
- Authorized to ask the assistant to go to the store to purchase more ingredients if running out
- Authorized to…

Table 3 - Sample Role Description-Responsibility-Authority Matrix

Step 3.5 - Determine Your Project's Non-Human Resource Requirements

Outline

Categories of Non-Human Resources
Initial Estimation of Non-Human Resources
Detailed Estimation of Non-Human Resources
Case Studies – Non-Human Resources

Introduction

You need to ensure that non-human resources are available for your project. You need sufficient funds to support non-human resources. What types of non-human resources do you need for your project? How do you determine how much money you need for the project's non-human resources?

Categories of Non-Human Resources

The following is a list of categories of non-human resources you might need for your project. Examples and or explanations are provided for each category.

- Tools - you need to get the project completed
- Equipment – you need to get the project completed

- Technology – laptop, printer, online subscription
- Data / Information / Knowledge (DIK)
- Materials – Fence posts, nails, pickets
- Office Supplies – Pens, pencils, printer paper, ink for the printer, stapler
- Real Estate Lease/Mortgage – for a property you lease or own where work is performed
- Utilities – gas, water, electricity
- Communication – cell phones, mobile service, phone service
- Furniture / Fixtures – desk, chair
- Sub-contracts - a graphic designer you hire to create a specific deliverable

Initial Estimation of Non-Human Resources

Decisions of moving forward or not with a project are usually made before you can prepare an accurate budget. Before you break down a project into its many components. So you need to estimate based on past experience and anything else you can get your hands on.

Detailed Estimation of Non-Human Resources

Define the non-human resources needed to complete each activity and/or sub-activity. Define any non-human resources needed to achieve any deliverable or sub-deliverable. Remove any duplicate resources.

Case Studies - Non-Human Resources

Fence Project – Non-Human Resources

Type	Name	Available?	Number of Units
Tool	Hammer	Yes	1
Equipment	Auger	No	1
Material	Nails (270 unit pkg)	N	5
Material	Bracket	N	26 x 6 brackets per post = 156 brackets
Material	Post – 4x4x10	N	26
Material	Rail – 2x4x8	N	25 sections x 3 rails=75
Material	Picket – 6ft x 0.6in	N	400

Nail Calculation:

6 nails per picket (to attach to 3 rails) x 400 pickets = 2400

2 nails per bracket to attach to post x 156 brackets = 312

4 nails per rail (to attach to 2 brackets) x 75 rails = 300

Total of above = About 3,000 nails, which is just over 11 packages, so purchase 12 packages.

SCD for Life Project – Non-Human Resources

Type	Name	Available?	Number of Units
Equipment	Stove	Yes	1
Equipment	Large Pot	Yes	1
Material	Chicken	N	5
Material	Carrots	N	20
Material	Eggs	N	<1 dozen
Material	Apples	N	10
Material	Beef Gelatin	N	½ cup

Step 3.6 - Determine Your Project's Costs and Budget

Outline

Why Estimate the Costs in More Detail?
Should You Hide Revised Cost Estimates?
How to Determine Cost of Human Resources?
Case Studies – Cost of Human Resources
How to Determine Cost of Non-Human Resources?
Case Studies – Cost of Non-Human Resources
Reserves

Why Estimate the Costs in More Detail?

You have already provided an initial cost estimate when preparing the Business Case (Step 1.2). Why should you refine this cost estimate further during the planning Step (Step 3)?

You now know much more about the project's requirements and updated scope (Step 3.1). You have by now defined a comprehensive mapping of the deliverables and activities for your project (Step 3.2). You have also defined your human resources (Step 3.4) and non-human resources (Step 3.5) in more detail. For all these reasons, you know so much more about your project than you did when creating the Business Case.

You should therefore adjust your costs to make them more realistic. Suppose the costs are going to be much less than originally anticipated. In that case, you might be able to re-direct them to another project that may benefit you, your career, or your business. If the costs are going to be higher than planned, you need to look into your pockets to make sure you can handle these increased costs. Otherwise, you should scale down the project given your existing budget or cancel the project altogether.

Should You Hide Revised Cost Estimates?

No! But I realize that there are situations when the costs are lower or higher than in the original Business Case, and project managers or management hide the change from their superiors for various reasons (in corporate or government settings). I also realize you are less likely to do that if the project is personal in nature or is for your own business. I do not condone this practice but understand the reality out there in the real world.

How to Determine Cost of Human Resources?

Some are human resources paid hourly, and others are paid a salary. To estimate total human resource costs, do the following:

Let's assume people work 2080 hours per year (40 hours per week for 52 weeks). For each person receiving a salary + benefits of $X/Year (that is, $X is the cost to you, not the pay to them), you can therefore estimate how much they cost you per hour.

For example, if Linda is an employee and costs your organization $110,000/year (total costs including salary and benefits), this is equivalent to $110,000 / 2080 = $52.89 per hour. If she is scheduled to work for 80 hours on the project, she will be paid a total of about $52.89 x 80 = $4,231 for the project.

And, if Joe is an independent contractor getting paid $50/hr and he is scheduled to work for 30 hours total on your project, then he will be paid $50 x 30 = $1,500.

If these are the only resources for your project, then the total cost of human resources for your project would be $1,500 + $4,231 = $5,731

Case Studies – Cost of Human Resources

In the case of the two case studies we have been following in this book, my wife and I spent our own time on these projects, we could establish how much our time is worth based on how much money we make from our real estate brokerage each year, and then divide the amount by 2080 hours to come up with an hourly rate, but this is not a practical thing to do since the Diet project was an emergency project, and we would not replace ourselves with "cheaper" resources to do the work, and the other Fence project was a "recreational" project, and I would not want anyone else to take away my fun of building the fence. You too will have many projects that you will want to handle yourself for various reasons, and accounting for human resource costs will not apply.

How to Determine Cost of Non-Human Resources?

Previously in Step 3.5, you established, in great detail, the various non-human resources involved in your project. You specified what each resource is and the quantity of that resource you need.

You should investigate each item's cost, multiply by the quantity, arrive at the total cost for the item, and then add all items' total costs to a grand total of non-human resource costs.

Case Studies – Cost of Non-Human Resources

Let's get back to the two case studies we are following in this book and calculate the total non-human resource costs for each one.

Fence Project – Non-Human Resource Costs					
Type	Name	Available?	Cost/Unit	Number of Units	Total Cost
Tool	Hammer	Y	/	/	/
Equipment	Auger	1	$300	1	$300
Material	Nails packages	N	$5	12	$60
Material	Bracket	N	$0.57	156	$89
Material	Post – 4x4x10	N	$16	26	$416
Material	Rail – 2x4x8	N	$8	75	$600
Material	Picket – 6ft x 0.6in	N	$2.32	400	$928
Sub-Total Non-Human Resources					$2,393

Tax (About 10%)					$239
Delivery			$75	2 Deliveries (some materials from Lowes and others from Home Depot)	$150
Total Non-Human Resources					$2,782

SCD for Life Project - Non-Human Resource Costs

Type	Name	Available?	Cost/Unit	Number of Units	Total Cost
Equipment	Stove	Yes	/	/	/
Equipment	Large Pot	Yes	/	/	/
Material	Chicken (organic)	N	$35/2 chicken package in Costco	1	$25

Material	Carrots	N	$4/bag of about 20	20	$4
Material	Eggs	N	$6/Dozen	<1 dozen	$6
Material	Apples (organic)	N	$2.5/lb	20 apples (7 lb)	/
Material	Beef Gelatin	N	$29 per 1lb package	<1 lb	$29
Sub-Total Non-Human Resources					$64
Tax (About 10%)					$6.4
Delivery					$0 (have Amazon prime)
Total Non-Human Resources					$70.4 (clearly, the costs are negligible, especially given the critical nature of the project)

Reserves

People tend to underestimate how much time activities take (and therefore the cost of human resources), as well as other non-human resource costs. It is best to include a reserve in your project's budget.

You should consider adding 5-10% on top of the specific costs you have identified for the project. You can add them as one number to the total cost of human resources as well as one number to the total cost of non-human resources. Alternatively, you can spread them throughout the project by adding 5-10% to individual activities and sub-activities.

Step 3.7 - Determine the Risks Involved in Your Project and Responses to Them

Outline

> Why Focus on Risk?
> How to Identify Risks?
> How to Record Risks?
> Case Studies – Risk Identification
> How to Assess Risks?
> How to Record Risk Assessment?
> Case Studies – Risk Assessment
> How to Define Risk Responses?
> How to Record Risk Responses?
> Case Studies – Risk Responses

Why Focus on Risk?

There is a risk to anything in life. A risk that one crosses the road and gets hit by a car, a risk that one goes to sleep and does not wake up again in the morning and on and on.

It is wise to manage risk in every aspect of your life. Crossing the road at sidewalks may be safer, eating healthy foods may increase your chances of waking up in the mornings more times than otherwise, and so on.

Unexpected situations may occur at any moment in your life and the life of your projects. They may result in increased costs, project delays, and sometimes in project termination.

How to Identify Risks?

The first step is to identify as many risks as possible to do with your project.

Ways to identify risks include:
- Recall your previous related experiences and think of what risks you faced.
- Ask the various stakeholders you have identified to-date for the project about what risks they see with the overall project or with just their portion of the project. It is a good idea to get multiple opinions.
- Research to find out what others have written about risks involved in similar situations.

How to Record Risks?

You may want to record the risks in a table such as the one below (see Table 4). Note that the Activity ID field is the ID you assigned to each activity previously in the WBS and that the Risk ID is a unique identifier you should assign for each risk identified (1,2,3…).

Activity ID	Risk ID	Description of Risk

Table 4 - Project Risks Table

Case Studies – Risk Identification

I went through each activity in the WBS and identified the risks that may be associated with each such activity. Below are partial lists (sufficient I hope to pass on the point of how to go about creating these tables).

Fence Project – List of Risks

Activity ID	Risk ID	Risk
2.1.2	1	Purchase insufficient amount of materials
2.1.2	2	Purchase too many materials
2.1.4	3	Some of the materials supposed to be delivered, not delivered
2.3.4	4	The new auger does not work once assembled
3.1.1	5	Roots of bushes next to fence location prevent the auger from digging further down
5.2.1	6	Hammer hits the fingers while hammering nails to connect brackets to posts

...	...	...

SCD for Life Project – List of Risks

Activity ID	Risk ID	Risk
1.2.1	1	Include an illegal food in the legal foods list
1.3.1	2	Include a legal food in the illegal foods list
2.1.1.4	3	Cut finger while peeling carrots
4.1.1 and 2.1.1.8	4	Boiling chicken soup spills on me while removing the pot from the stove
4.3.1 and 2.3.1.2	5	You burn your hand while lifting a hot handle of the apple sauce pot.
...	...	...

How to Assess Risks?

The second step is to assess each risk:
- Estimate the **Impact**, extent of the consequences. How much of the project will be affected if the risk materializes (happens)?

- **Probability** of the risk materializing. How likely is the risk to materialize (high, medium, low)? How often?

How to Record Risk Assessment?

You may want to record the assessment of the risks in a table such as the one below (see Table 5). Note that the RISK ID is the same as the ones you recorded in the previous table. The probability can be divided into several categories: Very Low, Low, Medium, High, Very High. Or just: Low, Medium, High. In the Impact field, you should detail the impact of the risk on the project should the risk materialize. You can also classify impact as Low, Medium, and High if you like.

Risk ID	Probability	Impact

Table 5 – Risk Probability and Impact Assessment Table

Case Studies – Risk Assessment

Fence Project – Risk Assessment

Risk ID	Probability	Impact
1	Medium	Low - No delay to project if insufficient materials. Can start project anyways,

		and request additional delivery. There will be the cost of extra materials and delivery.
2	Medium	Low - No delay to project if extra materials. Save the extra materials for future project(s).
3	Low	Low - No delay to project. Can get started anyway. Call the supplier and complain about missing materials, and deliver asap.
4	Low	High - Delay of the project if auger does not work. Delay may be 1-2 weeks.
5	High	Medium - Delay in hole digging since we will not be able to use auger.
…	…	…

SCD for Life Project – Risk Assessment

Risk ID	Probability	Impact
1	Low	High – illegal food, if consumed, can worsen the baby's condition and unnecessarily stop our SCD Diet trial (stage 0).
2	Low	Low - No impact in the short term if the baby does not eat food that is legal, other

		than them having less variety which would be unfortunate.
3	Low	Low – 5-minute delay to bandage finger. Not likely to happen as we are experienced with peeling…!
4	Low	High – you may need to be hospitalized and operated on if the burns are severe/extensive
5	Low	High – you may need to be hospitalized and operated on if the burns are severe/extensive
…	…	…

How to Define Risk Responses?

The third step requires developing a plan to minimize risk and/or protect the project from the risk consequences. You need to decide which risks you want to handle now, handle later, or only handle if they materialize.

Your options for handling risk include:
- Act to eliminate the risk
- Transfer the risk. For example, pay a third party to assume certain risk by purchasing insurance
- Act to reduce the likelihood the risk will occur
- Act to minimize the consequences of the risk if it does occur.
- Some combination of the above

Handling risks costs money and time (which is also money), So you need to decide if to makes sense to handle the risk or not.

Later on, when the project starts, you will need to:
- Monitor the project for risks throughout the project.
- Inform others about risks
- Communicate about the risk as soon as you determine it
- Request help others that may/could/should be able to help you

How to Record Risk Responses?

Enter this information in the risk response table below (Table 6).

Risk ID	Risk Response

Table 6 - Risk Response Table

Case Studies – Risk Responses

Fence Project – Risk Responses

Risk ID	Risk Response

1	Calculate materials three times before ordering.
2	Calculate materials three times before ordering.
3	Nothing to do at this time. If an item(s) is missing from the delivery, call the supplier to deliver the missing items.
4	Nothing to do at this time. Will need to call the supplier and request a new auger. Will also need to ship the broken auger back. Another option will be to dig the holes manually with a shovel and request a refund from the supplier.
5	Nothing to do at this time. Will need to cut roots manually. May need to spend a few extra hours cutting roots with manual tools.
6	
…	…

SCD for Life Project – Risk Responses

Risk ID	Risk Response
1	Spend additional hours researching the internet about what is legal and what is not. Double and triple check people's responses. If someone says a certain food is legal, check with multiple other people to ensure it is legal in their experiences as well.
2	Nothing to do at this time beyond what will be done to respond to risk #1 above.

3	Wear one-time kitchen gloves while peeling carrots so that there is a barrier between the peeler and the skin.
4	Wear oven mitts while handling the pot.
5	Wear oven mitts while handling the pot.
…	…

Step 3.8 - Define Project Communication

Outline

What is Communication?
Why Plan the Communication Related to Your Project?
The Communication Process
How is Communication Handled?
How Can Written Communication be Conducted?
How Frequently Should Communication Take Place?
Create a Communication Plan for Your Project
Case Studies – Communication Plan

What is Communication?

Communication is sending and receiving Data, Information and/or Knowledge (DIK) to share meaning and achieve goals. Communication can be verbal or non-verbal.

Why Plan the Communication Related to Your Project?

Project team members and other stakeholders internal and external to your organization may need to interact with one another throughout the implementation.

The Communication Process

The communication process consists of a sender, a message, a communication channel, and a receiver.

The communication process consists of the following components (see Figure 13):
- Message
- Sender
- Encoded Message
- Communication channel (can be more or less formal)
- Noise
- Receiver
- Decoded Message
- Feedback

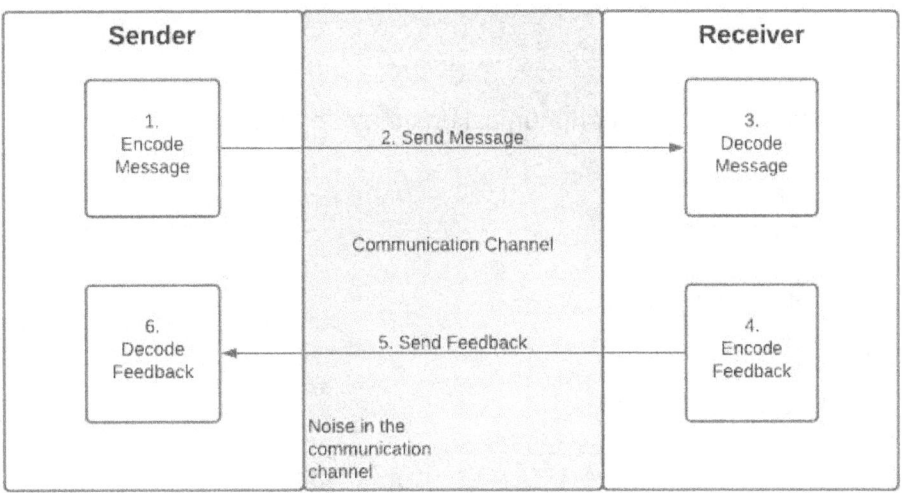

Figure 13 - The Communication Process

The communications process consists of the following steps:
1. The sender encodes the message
2. The sender sends the message through a communication channel
3. The receiver decodes the message
4. The receiver encodes feedback for the sender
5. The receiver of the initial message sends the feedback to the original message's sender through a communication channel.
6. The sender of the original message decodes the message

Effective communication involves the following:
- Listening
- Asking questions
- Clarity of message

How is Communication Handled?

Various channels of communications may be employed:

- Email
- Text
- In-person meeting
- Zoom meeting
- Social Media Post
- Website Update

In larger, more formal projects, a significant portion of the communication is done in writing.

How Can Written Communication be Conducted?

Written Communication can be:

- Created
- Reviewed
- Presented
- Executed (signed)
- Distributed
- Stored
- Updated

Documents may include:

- Reports (Various formats: MSWord, PDF)
- Presentations (PowerPoint)
- Charts (PDF)
- Spreadsheets (Excel)
- Databases containing DIK

How Frequently Should Communication Take Place?

Documents may be created/distributed on a schedule:

- Daily
- Weekly
- Monthly
- Before meetings
- Following meetings
- At the start of each deliverable
- At the end of each deliverable
- At specific project milestones

Examples of documents:

- The various documents we discussed thus far in this book
- Log of issues
- Project performance data

Create a Communication Plan for Your Project

Look at each activity, sub-activity, deliverable, and sub-deliverable and define who will communicate with whom, how, and when (See Table 7)

Sender	Receiver	Message	Channel	Frequency

Table 7 - Project Communication Plan

You can optionally include Activity ID / Deliverable ID as an added field in larger / more formal projects.

Case Studies – Communication Plan

Examples for our two projects:

Fence Project – Communication Plan

Sender	Receiver	Message	Channel	Frequency
David	Orit	Check out the progress!	Meeting at the site	Daily

David	Orit	Need more $	Email	As needed when about to incur an unexpected expense
...	...	...		

SCD for Life Project – Communication Plan

Sender	Receiver	Message	Channel	Frequency
Orit	David	Info about SCD Diet	Meeting	As new info uncovered
Orit	David	Info about SCD Diet	Email	As new info uncovered
Orit	David	Request to print documents	Email	As information gets updated (Orit has a problem connecting to the printer, so I get to print things for her)
David	Orit	Inform document printed	Email	Each time Orit requests David to print a document
David	Orit	Provide hardcopy document	In-Person	Each David prints a document for Orit
...	...	...	...	...

Step 3.9 - Define Project Procurement

Outline

>   What Is Procurement?
>   Who is Involved in Procurement?
>   The Steps Involved in the Procurement Process
>   More About Procurement
>   Request for Quotation (RFQ)
>   Request for Proposal (RFP)
>   Request for Information (RFI)
>   Inform Vendors About Your RFQ / RFP / RFI
>   Receive and Evaluate Responses from Vendors
>   Negotiate the Contract with Vendors and Assign Work

What Is Procurement?

Larger and or more formal projects may involve buying a product, service, or DIK from a vendor outside your organization.

Who is Involved in Procurement?

Governmental organizations, financial sector organizations, public companies all engage in formal procurement practices. They are likely to have procurement departments. Anyone can, however, engage in formal or informal procurement.

Your vendors may also be referred to as sellers, contractors, sub-contractors, service providers, or suppliers.

In some situations, your project may involve you selling a product, service, or DIK to an outside organization.

Your buyers may be referred to as customers, clients, purchasers, or service requesters.

The Steps Involved in the Procurement Process

You need to define what you want to purchase, sell, lease from, lease to.

You need to create a plan for how you will go about purchasing, selling, or leasing this product, service, or DIK.

The process includes:

- Define terms
- Identify potential clients or suppliers (or however you choose to refer to them)
- Propose terms
- Negotiate terms
- Review terms

- Create contract
- Review contract
- Negotiate contract

More About Procurement

Contracts are legal documents requiring more thinking, analysis, review, and approvals than other reports created as part of a project.

Other organizations face decisions if to buy or create in-house or outsource the work to outside organizations.

Request for Quotation (RFQ)

Once you know what you want to outsource to a vendor, if your decision will be based on price and you know exactly what you need, you will create and issue a **Request for Quotation (RFQ)**.

Request for Proposal (RFP)

If your decision will be made on more than just the price, and you want to evaluate each vendor's merits, you should create and issue a document known as a **Request for Proposals (RFP)**.

Request for Information (RFI)

Suppose you need some information at a certain stage and want to find out how different vendors will handle your situation or solve your problem. In that case, you will create and issue a document known as a **Request for Information (RFI)**.

Inform Vendors About Your RFQ / RFP / RFI

You can inform specific vendors about your opportunities and provide them with deadlines to respond to you. You can call, text, or email vendors to let them know about the opportunity and see if they would like to look at the full details of your RFP, RFQ, or RFI.

You might want them to sign a confidentiality and non-disclosure agreement before you provide them the full details.

You can also post your opportunities on Freelancer dot com, Fiverr dot com, or many other general or industry-specific websites.

You should provide a specific deadline for responses. The larger the project and the more complex the response is expected to be, the more time you might want to give vendors to respond.

Receive and Evaluate Responses from Vendors

Once the deadline passes, you should review the responses to your RFQ / RFP / RFI. You can ask vendors for clarifications for more details as needed.

At a certain stage, you should also decide if you wish to proceed with any of the vendors and which vendor(s) you wish to proceed with.

Negotiate the Contract with Vendors and Assign Work

Next, you might want to negotiate further with one or more specific vendors, sign agreements with the vendor(s) for them to deliver the desired outcomes (products, services, DIK), and proceed to assign the work.

Step 3.10 - Define Stakeholder Engagement

Outline

Why is Engaging Stakeholders Important throughout Your Project?
What's the Goal of Stakeholder Engagement Planning?
Which Stakeholders Should be Engaged?
Assess Stakeholder Power and Interest Level Before Planning Stakeholder Engagement
Possible Engagement Statuses
Document Current and Target Engagement Statuses
Define When to Start Engaging Each Stakeholder
Define How to Engage Each Stakeholder
Define How Often to Engage Each Stakeholder
Case Studies – Stakeholder Engagement Status

Why is Engaging Stakeholders Important throughout Your Project?

You want to identify people, groups, organizations that could impact your project. You want to analyze and understand their position towards the project and develop a strategy to bring them from their starting engagement status to a desired engagement status.

Stakeholder engagement at its core consists of ongoing communication, as discussed earlier in Step 3.8.

What's the Goal of Stakeholder Engagement Planning?

Bring each stakeholder from their current engagement status to the engagement status you desire for them.

Which Stakeholders Should be Engaged?

Start with planning the engagement of each of the stakeholders you identified for your project previously in Step 2.2. Remove any stakeholders which you previously identified that no longer have an impact on your project. Review the remaining stakeholders and update whatever relevant information you learned about them since the start of the project planning. Finally, add to this list any additional stakeholders you identified since then.

Assess Stakeholder Power and Interest Level Before Planning Stakeholder Engagement

It's important to assess your stakeholders' power and interest level. And there are four general categories:

- those that have low power and low interest require minimal effort
- those that have low power but high interest should be kept informed
- those that have high power and low interest need to be kept satisfied

- and those that have high power and high interest need to be managed closely

You can record this information in a table such as this (See Table 8)

Stakeholder Name	Stakeholder Role	Power Level	Interest Level

Table 8 - Stakeholder Power and Interest

Possible Engagement Statuses

The options are:
- Unaware – you believe or know for a fact that the stakeholder is not aware of the project.
- Resistant – you believe or know for a fact that the stakeholder is against the whole project or part of the project and is resistant to the change that the project will bring.
- Neutral – to your knowledge, the stakeholder is aware of the project, but you are not aware that they have expressed any opinion, pro or

against the project. You are not aware that they are resistant to the change the project will bring.
- Supportive – you believe or know that the stakeholder has expressed support for the project and the changes the project will bring.
- Leading – you believe or know that the stakeholder will actively help you with the efforts related to your project to bring about the change.

Next, you should define what relationship you need to have with each category of stakeholder. Communication with clients, for example, would be different than with your team members implementing your project. Defining and documenting each type of relationship will create clarity for you and them and reduce the likelihood of problems during the project.

Document Current and Target Engagement Statuses

Add two new columns to your stakeholder list (Table above): Current Engagement Status and Target Engagement Status.

Your Stakeholder Engagement information can be organized as follows (See Table 10):

Stakeholder Name	...	Current Engagement Status	Target Engagement Status
Stakeholder 1		Resistant	Supportive
Stakeholder 2		Supportive	Leading

Stakeholder 3		Unaware	Neutral
...			

Table 9 - Stakeholder Engagement - Current and Target

Define When to Start Engaging Each Stakeholder

For each category of stakeholder, decide when to start involving them in the project:

- At the start of the Evaluation
- At the start of the Initiation
- At the start of Planning
- At the start of the Implementation
- At the end of the Implementation
- At some other point

Define How to Engage Each Stakeholder

For each category of stakeholder, define the ways to communicate with them about the project:

- one on one meetings
- group meetings
- informal written correspondence

- formal information sharing
- written approval

Define How Often to Engage Each Stakeholder

You can engage your stakeholders:

- Daily
- Weekly
- Monthly
- Just before an intermediate deliverable is finalized
- Once an intermediate deliverable has been finalized

The following format is suggested for recording when to start engaging each stakeholder, how and how often (See Table 10).

Stakeholder	When to Start Engaging?	How to Engage?	How often to Engage?

Table 10 - Stakeholder Engagement Schedule

Case Studies – Stakeholder Engagement Status

Rather than show you stakeholder engagement status in tables, I will show you the same information in a bulleted format. In a more formal project, you might want to present this data in the tabular format proposed earlier in this step.

Fence Project – Stakeholder Engagement Status

Stakeholder: Orit
- Get her involved from the start. Need her blessing to proceed with spending an estimated $2,500. Without her, there is no project

Stakeholder: Home Depot delivery person
- Will get involved on the day of delivery
- Will need to text him info about where to deliver the materials

Stakeholder: David
- I talk to myself all the time… ☺

SCD for Life Project – Stakeholder Engagement Status

Stakeholder: Orit
- She talks to herself from time to time

Stakeholder: David
- Orit tells me what to do all the time… ☺

- Get involved from the start

Stakeholder: Medical Doctor Promoting SCD
- Email him and then speak with him
- Involved as soon as Orit bought and read the book he wrote

Stakeholder: SCD Consultant
- Phone consultation as soon as joined the FB group
- Email exchanges moving forward
- FB posts – question/answer format moving forward

Stakeholder: SCD Advisers
- FB posts – question/answer format
- Involved as soon as Orit joined the FB group

Stakeholder: Medical Doctors Promoting Drugs
- Request feedback on child's condition each time there is a change in condition
- Provide feedback on the progress of diet, in case they want to share with other patients

Stakeholder: coordinator of the SCD group on Facebook
- Involved as soon as Orit discovered the SCD group
- Provided Orit with an outline of the SCD diet and keys to the successful implementation of this diet

Stakeholder: mothers that are part of the SCD Facebook group
- Involved as soon as Orit discovered the SCD group
- Interaction via Q&A in the FB SCD Group

Stakeholder: the doctors at UCLA Medical Center, Cedar Sinai Medical Center, and Harvard University/Boston Children's Hospital that have been involved in our child's care pre-SCD adoption
- Involved in the ongoing care of our child since before trying SCD.
- Orit keeps them updated via email

Stakeholder: Chron's and Colitis Foundation of America (CCFA) staff
- Involved since before trying SCD.
- Ask for contact with others that have implemented SCD.

Stakeholder: CCFA volunteers
- Involved since before trying SCD.
- Ask for contact with others that have implemented SCD.

Step 3.11 - Define the Quality of Project Deliverables and Activities

Outline

What is Quality in the Context of Project Management?

The Costs of Managing the Quality of the Activities and Deliverables of Your Project

The Benefits of Managing the Quality of the Activities and Deliverables of Your Project

What can you do to Increase the Quality of Your Project's Activities and Deliverables?

The Quality Requirements for Your Project

What is Quality Assurance?

What is Quality Control?

What is Continuous Process Improvement?

Identify Quality Requirements

Create Quality Checklists

Define Quality Matrices

What is Quality in the Context of Project Management?

In project management, when we talk about quality, we think about how to make the deliverables as beneficial as possible to the people (stakeholders) that need them but also how to make the process of getting to these final deliverables as effective as possible for those (other stakeholders including team members) involved in the process.

The Costs of Managing the Quality of the Activities and Deliverables of Your Project

Ensuring your project's activities are performed to higher standards to the stakeholders' benefit means more planning. It also requires testing / measuring the activities as they are executed to ensure the plan's quality standards are being implemented. Finally, it requires adjustments to the activities if the results of testing/measuring indicate that activity changes/improvements are needed.

In parallel, you need to look at the intermediate deliverables your project produces and test/measure if these deliverables are to the stakeholders' standards. If this is not the case, you need to make adjustments to the activities to get there.

All of this takes time and money to plan, test/measure, and adjust your project to progress at a certain quality and deliver desired quality outcomes.

This time and money come on top of the time and money you need to implement the project if you did not consider the quality-related matters.

So why take extra time and money and consider the quality of your projects? Since there are short- and long-term benefits in managing the quality of your projects. Some benefits are provided during the project, and other benefits are revealed only once the project is complete and stakeholders use the project's outcomes.

The Benefits of Managing the Quality of the Activities and Deliverables of Your Project

Benefits of managing the quality of your projects may include:

- Happier team members that are more focused and produce better results.
- Intermediate deliverables that satisfy your clients/customers
- Catching errors in your project's activities sooner than later during your projects means fixing them is quicker and less costly
- The final deliverables are more likely to accomplish what the stakeholders wanted, and you have less conflict and with fewer people

- Less likely to have the project canceled mid-way
- Less likely to get sued by unhappy customers
- Less likely to get your and your organization's reputation damaged or destroyed

What can you do to Increase the Quality of Your Project's Activities and Deliverables?

Some of the things you can do to increase the quality of your project's activities and deliverables:

- Provide training to certain team members
- Provide more training to those trained
- Provide clearer instructions
- Provide more detailed documentation on how to perform certain activities
- Provide more time to perform certain activities
- Provide equipment / better equipment to perform certain activities
- Provide a better work environment
- Perform more testing/evaluations of the activities
- Perform more testing/evaluations of the intermediate deliverables

People often confuse quality assurance and quality control. Let's look at these two terms next.

The Quality Requirements for Your Project

You get to define the quality of your project's final deliverable, as well as the quality of its activities and intermediate deliverables. Ideally, you should define the quality of a project through consultations with the project's various stakeholders. If you are not the owner/sponsor of the project, then, of course, you should get their blessing before you finalize the project's quality requirements.

What is Quality Assurance?

Quality Assurance is what you or others do to prevent problems/defects. For example, the project involves ten activities that must be completed in a certain order. You could create a **Checklist** listing the ten activities in the order in which they need to be performed and provide the checklist to the team member responsible for implementing these activities. As soon as your team member completes the first activity, they go to the checklist and place a checkmark next to the first activity. They then look at the activity listed below it and go ahead and implement that second activity. When done with the second activity, they go back to the checklist, mark the second activity as completed, and so on until they are done with all ten activities. Using such a checklist is one way to have your team member, not miss steps. By marking this checklist as they go, your team member is more likely to do a better job with the ten steps and thus more likely to produce a higher quality deliverable.

What is Quality Control?

Quality Control is what you or others do to identify problems/defects. Consider the previous example. You could do at least two things. First, you could verify that the checkmarks appear next to each item in the checklist. Second, you could conduct a test… take two of the ten activities, and review with your team member that they were completed correctly. By doing these things, you control the activities' quality, thus influencing the deliverables' quality resulting from the activities.

What is Continuous Process Improvement?

The idea here is that you need to plan and have your team execute quality-related initiatives throughout the project, from its start to its conclusion.

Quality needs to deal with the stakeholders' needs, the activities, the intermediate and final deliverables.

You can do many things to increase your processes' quality (working on the activities) and the quality of the intermediate and final deliverables. This book, which treats this topic at an introductory level, will look at a few basic things you can do.

Identify Quality Requirements

Identify quality requirements for deliverables and activities. You could record them in the following table (See Table 11):

Activity ID / Deliverable ID	Quality Requirement ID	Quality Requirement

Table 11 - Quality Requirements

Note that in the above table, the Activity IDs / Deliverable IDs were previously identified and recorded in Step 3.2.

Create Quality Checklists

A **Quality Checklist** lists a set of required steps to be performed to complete an activity (or sub-activity) or achieve a deliverable or a sub-deliverable. This list will need to be updated and reviewed during the implementation step by those team members performing the work as they perform it. You can review the checklist of your team members to verify that the required steps were performed.

You could create checklists formatted as follows (See Table 12)

Step #	Action to Perform	Action Performed?
1	Do this…	✓
2	Do that…	
3		

Table 12 - Quality Checklist Template

For example, I use a quality checklist when planting a new fruit tree in my backyard farm (I have a backyard farm with about 150 fruit trees, which originally come from various parts of the world). The checklist helps me ensure I do not miss any steps and correctly handle the planting of young fruit trees (See Table 13).

Step #	Action to Perform	Action Performed?
1	Bring Shovel to the location where the tree will be planted	✓
2	Bring a bag of planting soil to the location where the tree will be planted	
3	Dig hole that is 2 ft wide and 2 ft deep	
4	Make sure the hole is 2 ft wide and deep	
5	Remove the tree from the plastic container	
6	Place tree in the center of the hole	
7	Open planting soil bag and place soil in the hole around the tree	
8	Create a mound around the hole to hold water when watering	
9	Bring hose and water the plant	
10	Dispose of empty soil bag and a plastic container that held the tree	

Table 13 - Quality Checklist Example

Define Quality Matrices

A Quality Matrix describes a project or product attributes and how they will be measured.

Take a look at these two examples showing specific quality matrices. Each one shows a specific attribute and how to measure it. It also shows what action to take if it falls outside of the acceptable range:

- The number of bad nails (nails without heads) in a box of nails must be less than 10% of the box's total nails. If it is larger, call Home Depot to send you a new nail box at no extra charge. The way you would detect this situation is by visual inspection.
- Adjacent pickets of the fence should be installed at a similar height. The difference in height between any two adjacent pickets should not be greater than ¼ of an inch. If a picket is more than ¼ inch higher than the previous picket installed, remove the picket and re-install it. The way you would detect the situation is by visual inspection and a measuring tape if needed.

Such quality matrices can be used to perform both quality assurance and quality control in your projects. Again, there is so much more that can be said and done related to the quality of projects, but this is outside the introductory text's scope.

Step 3.12 - Plan Change Management

Outline

Change Is All-Around
Why is it Important to Embrace Change Management During Projects?
What is Project Change Management?
Create an Environment Where Change is Welcome
Create a Formal Change Request Process
Define the Change Request Form
Define How Change Requests are Approved or Rejected

Change Is All-Around

We live in a dynamic world where things are constantly changing. Much of the change is driven by advancements in technology (automation). New software with new pages and new buttons and new menus keep penetrating our lives and impacting them for the better and the worse.

An individual or family that does not embrace change is left behind and has a harder time competing for education, jobs, money, and for what you can buy with money if you have it.

Organizations (for-profit businesses, nonprofits, governments at local, regional, state, or national levels) that do not embrace change are left behind their competition and eventually maybe hurt or end their existence. Why is this so?

Since the competition that does embrace change can position itself better in a more competitive situation and thus provide better and cheaper products and services to its customers and take away customers from those organizations that are slower to embrace change.

Therefore, as you work on projects for yourself, for companies you work for or own, you must be flexible and adjust them during their duration to accommodate the changing competitive environment around you.

Why is it Important to Embrace Change Management During Projects?

When you start planning a project, you and possibly other stakeholders have a vision of what it will deliver and how it will work. Larger projects take time to initiate, plan and implement. These steps may take months and sometimes years. During that time, things may change, you, existing or new stakeholders may develop new and/or improved ideas for the project, its activities, and or deliverables. Your organization's competition may bring to the market new products, services, or DIK that will require changes to your project to deliver competitive results.

What is Project Change Management?

Project Change Management is the process of evaluating, initiating, planning, and implementing changes into a project.

Create an Environment Where Change is Welcome

You need to understand that change to project scope and other aspects of projects happen in the vast majority of projects. We live in a fast-changing world and need to be flexible in the way we handle things. You, as a project manager, should therefore prepare yourself mentally to embrace change.

You should also prepare the stakeholders involved in your project to understand that change to projects throughout their lifecycle is very likely to happen and why and accept this.

Therefore, in addition to planning the various aspects of the project we already discussed in this book, you should also create a plan on how to handle changes within your project.

You should create an environment where any project stakeholder can propose changes to projects.

A possible change request strategy is discussed next.

Create a Formal Change Request Process

If you own a project, you can, of course, do anything you want and make changes to the project throughout the project's duration.

Proposed changes should be formally reviewed for larger / more formal projects. You, along with the project's sponsor and/or owner, should define who will be responsible for reviewing and approving/denying change requests.

Possible stakeholders that can be tasked with review/approval of change requests include:

- You
- Your manager
- The project sponsor
- The project owner
- A committee specifically assigned for this with a representative from different departments
- A committee specifically assigned for this with a representation of different types of stakeholders
- Someone else (one or more stakeholders)

Define the Change Request Form

Create a form that needs to be filled in by anyone who wants to introduce change to the project. The form will need to be completed in its entirety and provided to you.

Your form can be a paper form or an online form and could include the following fields:

- Project Name
- Change Name

- Change ID
- Requested by
- Date of Change Request
- Reason for Change
- Change Priority (According to change proposer)
- Impact on activities
- Impact on deliverables
- Impact if change is not handled
- Estimated cost of proposed changes
- Estimated time needed to implement change
- HR Resources needed to implement change

There should be a place for reviewer comments. There should also be a place to indicate if a change is approved or denied and a place for signatures.

Define How Change Requests are Approved or Rejected

You should define a process to handle change requests. Your process may consist of the following steps:

1. A stakeholder fills in the change request form and submits it (paper or online)
2. The change request is recorded
3. The change request is reviewed by the individual(s) assigned to review change requests (as we discussed earlier in this chapter)

4. The change request is approved, denied, or a request for additional information/clarifications is made. If change is approved, proceed to the next steps.
5. Change project plans (the documents created in previous steps during the planning step)
6. Assigned work to your team
7. You will need to oversee the implementation of the change(s) to completion in addition to the other work already planned

Step 3.13 - Plan Larger and/or More Formal Projects: The Project Management Plan

Outline

What is the Project Management Plan?
Should a Project Management Plan be Created?
When Should the Project Management Plan be Created?
Can a Project Management Plan be Modified Once Approved?
What is the Difference Between the Project Management Plan and All the Other Documents We Discussed So Far in This Book?
What Should Be Included in the Project Management Plan?

Introduction

Please note that the creation of the Project Management Plan is a more advanced topic. It is recommended you read this chapter once and possibly 2-3 times. If you are not clear on this chapter, you might want to implement and manage your first few smaller projects without a Project Management Plan. Then once you are familiar with creating all other plans for your project (those discussed earlier in the book), you can come back to this chapter and try again.

What is the Project Management Plan?

The **Project Management Plan** is the primary document for your project! It is a document that defines how your project's work is to be managed. It also defines how the project's work is delegated, performed, controlled, and wrapped up. It can also define all project work that needs to be done (optional if you keep the work plans separate).

Should a Project Management Plan be Created?

You may consider not creating a Project Management Plan for relatively small projects in scope and duration.

For projects where you are not the sponsor and/or owner, you may be asked to create a Project Management Plan.

When Should the Project Management Plan be Created?

As you go through the planning of each of the nine components of a project (scope, schedule, HR, Cost, Risk, Communication, Procurement, Stakeholders, and Quality), you should also create a plan of how you would manage this aspect of the project later during the project's implementation (in Step 4).

These nine plans can be separate documents referred to in the Project Management Plan or included as chapters in such a plan.

You learned the steps for systematically running a project. You learned which documentation is advisable to create at each step of the way.

For larger projects, you might also consider creating a Project Management Plan. The creation of this management plan should start as soon as your project is approved based on the business case you present, and you move on to creating the project charter (so you start working on this document as soon as you enter the Initiation step).

You will also need to create a plan for Change Management as a separate document or chapter in the Project Management Plan.

You enhance the document further throughout the planning phase

Can a Project Management Plan be Modified Once Approved?

Yes! And it should be modified on an ongoing basis as changes are requested and then approved (we discussed the process in the previous section). The changes should be reflected in this Project Management Plan.

What is the Difference Between the Project Management Plan and all the Other Documents We Discussed So Far in this Book?

The next point is critical to understand so, read the next sentence as many times as needed until you understand it. **All other planning documents discuss <u>what needs to be done</u> to get the project completed, while the Project

Management Plan discusses <u>how the project will be managed</u> (by you) while the work is being done (by others). The Project Management Plan could include all other planning documents as sections in it but does not have to.

What Should be Included in the Project Management Plan?

The Project Management Plan **COULD** include all the deliverables you have created thus far in step 3 (or you can keep these previously created documents separate from the Project Management Plan:

- Project Stakeholders (defined in Step 2.2)
- Project Requirements (defined in Step 3.1)
- Project Scope (defined in Step 3.1)
- Project Deliverables (defined in Step 3.2)
- Project Activities (defined in Step 3.2)
- Ordered Activities (defined in Step 3.3)
- Activities-Resources-Durations (define in Step 3.3)
- Project Schedule (Defined in Step 3.3)
- Human Resources List (defined in Step 3.4)
- Roles-Responsibilities-Skills (defined in Step 3.4)
- Organization Chart (defined in Step 3.4)
- Project Non-Human Resources (defined in Step 3.5)
- Project Costs (defined in Step 3.6)
- Project Budget (define in Step 3.6)
- Project Risks (defined in Step 3.7)
- Project Responses to Risks (defined in Step 3.7)

- Project Communication Plan (defined in Step 3.8)
- Project Procurement Plan (defined in Step 3.9)
- Any RFPs / RFQs / RFIs (if you defined any in Step 3.9)
- Project Stakeholder Engagement Plan (defined in Step 3.10)
- Project Quality Requirements (defined in Step 3.11)
- Project Quality Tests (defined in Step 3.11)

You can take all of the above documents if you like or if you are instructed to do so by management and merge them into one document.

Your Project Management Plan **SHOULD** include:

- A detailed explanation of how work will be delegated (will be defined in Step 4.1)
- A detailed explanation of how work is to be performed by your team (will be defined in Step 4.2)
- A detailed explanation of how work is to be controlled (will be defined in Step 4.3)
- A detailed explanation of how the change will be introduced and controlled and how various plans will be modified to accommodate approved changes to your project (defined previously in Step 3.12)
- A detailed explanation of how the project will be wrapped up (will be defined in Step 4.4).

Step 4 – Implement

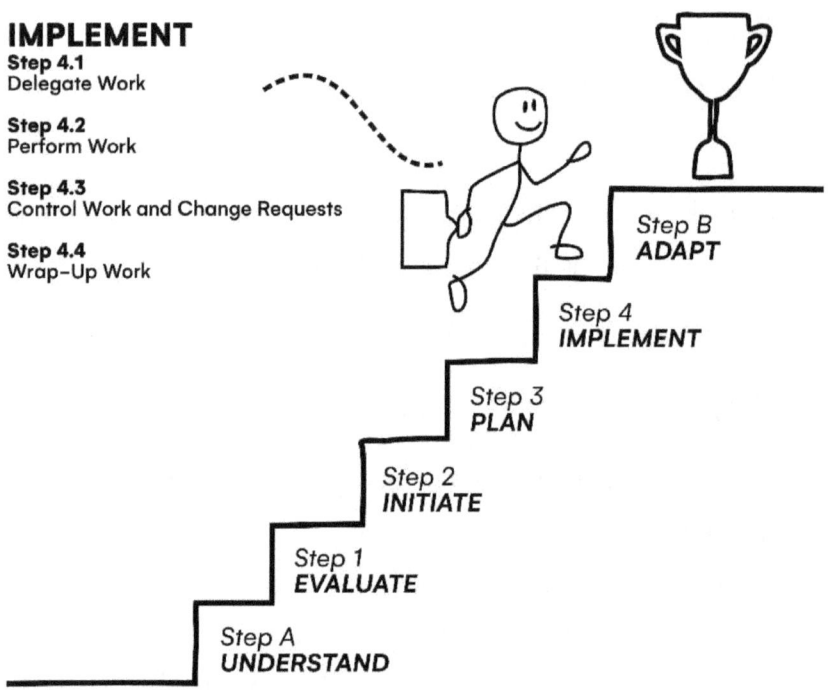

Step 4 - Overview

You will learn to delegate work, control work, and transition as work nears completion (we will not discuss how to do the actual work... that you will need to learn elsewhere, of course!).

Step 4 - Outline

      Step 4.1 - Delegate Work to Your Team
      Step 4.2 - Perform Work on the Project's Activities
      Step 4.3 - Control Your Project
      Step 4.4 - Wrap Up the Project

Step 4 - Objectives

You should be able to explain how to inform the team to get the work started

You Should be able to explain how to delegate work to your project team

You should be able to explain how to control the work of your project team

You should be able to explain how to handle wrapping up your project

Step 4.1 - Delegate Work to Your Team

Outline

What is Authority, Responsibility, and Accountability?
What is Delegation?
Why Delegate?
What to Delegate?
To What Extent Can You Delegate?
How to Delegate?
How to Hold People Accountable When You Don't Have Direct Authority Over Them?
What Roles Can You Assign?

What is Authority, Responsibility, and Accountability?

People don't know what's on your mind, what your goals are, what your expectations of them are.

Defining team members' roles and responsibilities are therefore critical to your and your project's success.

You should be aware of your own authority given the limitation defined previously while planning your project. **Authority** is the power you have, which may have been given to you, to define what you can and cannot do and what decisions you can and cannot make. For example, you have a limited amount of time or money to achieve a certain goal, as your manager informed you.

There are two additional terms you should bring to focus as a project manager. **Responsibility** is the duty to respond/take actions to achieve specific results, and **Accountability** is to account for achieving specific results!

What is Delegation?

Delegating is giving away something you have. It can mean shifting away authority, accountability, or responsibility for a particular activity or a part of the project.

It is important to understand why delegation is often key to success. It is also important to know what to delegate and what not to delegate, and to what degree.

Why Delegate?

You should consider delegating work to others in the following situations:
- If you want or need to free your time to do something else
- If you want or need someone more qualified to handle the job
- To get a qualified person's opinion on an issue
- To teach someone to do something

What to Delegate?

You should consider delegating work that:
- Others can handle it better, quicker, etc.
- You have clearly defined

To What Extent Can You Delegate?

You can delegate work to different extents:
- Delegate actions to implement something specific (do as I say)
- Delegate research about a topic (look into this)
- Delegate developing options about a situation (provide me advice, and I will decide)
- Delegate to decide what to do, let me know what you are going to do, and then it unless I stop you midway (investigate, decide and check with me before implementing)
- Investigate, decide and implement if within these limits
- Delegate everything from start to finish. Just let me know how it went.
- Delegate dealing with the situation (deal with it).

How to Delegate?

The steps to delegate work to others are:
- Clarify what you want to delegate
- Choose the right person
- Explain the activity
- Be available to answer questions
- Monitor performance
- Address problems as they arise

How to Hold People Accountable When You Don't Have Direct Authority Over Them?

The following are some of the things you can do to hold people accountable when you do not have direct authority over them:
- Find out who is the person's manager and bring them to the process
- Put in in writing
- Be specific
- Follow-up
- Make the person accountable to the team
- Get commitment
- Create a sense of urgency and importance

What Roles Can You Assign?

You can assign any of the following roles to stakeholders involved in your project:
- Primary responsibility – Person responsible for handling all or a majority of an activity
- Secondary responsibility – Person responsible for a relatively minor aspect of an activity
- Approval – Person responsible for approval of an activity
- Review – Person responsible for the review of an activity
- Input – Person responsible for providing input to an activity
- Output – Person responsible for presenting the output of the activity

For each person, you will have involved in the project, determine their roles for each activity. Review their roles with them, and get their understanding and agreement.

Step 4.2 - Perform Work on the Project's Activities

Outline

When Should You Get the Work Started?
How to Inform Stakeholders That Work is Starting?
What to Do When Starting Work with Your Team?

When Should You Get the Work Started?

Once the project is approved, you, the project manager, should inform all stakeholders that work is about to start.

How to Inform Stakeholders That Work is Starting?

You can share some information during a team meeting and other information during one-on-one meetings. These days the various meetings can be conducted via zoom or another similar technology.

What to Do When Starting Work with Your Team?

You should do the following with your team members:
- Re-confirm their participation
- Review individual and team goals with each member
- Review the role of each member

- Review the various documents created during the planning phase. Each team member should be given access to only those documents that you feel are relevant to their role in the project.
- Review operating procedures to do with
    - Communication
    - Decision making
    - Conflict resolution
    - Change management
- Review timelines
- Review relationships with other members

And then, announce the formal start of the project!

Step 4.3 - Control Your Project

Outline

- What is Controlling a Project?
- How to Control a Project?
- Maintain Control by Tracking Progress
- Maintain Control by Comparing Progress to Plans
- Maintain Control Through Effective Change Request Management Procedures
- Maintain Control Through Effective Communication to Minimize Conflict and Optimize Performance
- About Meetings
- Maintain Control Through Effective Leadership to Optimize Performance
- Key Characteristics of a Leader
- Why People Do What They Are Asked to Do?
- How Can you Establish Your Leadership?
- Maintaining Control Through Effective Stakeholder Engagement

What is Controlling a Project?

The goal of controlling a project is to ensure that the project's goals are achieved by implementing your project according to your plans.

How to Control a Project?

The key things you can do to control a project are:
- Maintain control by tracking progress
- Maintain control by comparing progress to plans
- Maintain control through effective change request management procedures
- Maintain control through effective communication to minimize conflict and optimize performance
- Maintain control through effective leadership to optimize performance
- Maintain control through effective stakeholder engagement

These are discussed in the next few sections.

Maintain Control by Tracking Progress

To maintain control of your project, you need to be able to track its overall progress, as well as the progress of individual activities.

This includes:
- Monitoring deliverable dates
- Monitoring the progress of work on activities
- Evaluating performance relative to plans
- Monitoring human resources
- Taking corrective action
- Keeping team members and other stakeholders informed
- Monitoring non-human resource expenditures

Some things should be monitored daily, others weekly, and for longer projects, monthly is also an option.

Maintain Control by Comparing Progress to Plans

You should track performance and compare it to its baseline (your original plans for the project). Comparing frequently and regularly is very important. It is a way to catch issues as soon as they arise.

Evaluate the project's financial performance by comparing actual expenditures with planned expenditures. Ask yourself the following questions:

- On target?
- Are you over budget?
- Under budget?
- What can you do to improve?

You should continually work to identify possible causes of delays, as well as possible corrective actions.

Sometimes a delay may correct itself. Sometimes you will need to adjust the original approved plans. If there are stakeholders above you, you will need to explain to them why this adjustment is necessary. Once you have approval, you can inform your team of the adjusted dates, requirements, etc.

Maintain Control Through Effective Change Request Management Procedures

As projects progress, they often have changes introduced to them by stakeholders.

Here are the steps to handle changes during project implementation:
- You receive a request to incorporate a change in your project from a stakeholder (this could be you)
- Ask for a written confirmation of the request (in larger projects, there may be a formal change request form)
- Assess the potential impact on the project
- Decide if to implement the change
- If you decide not to implement, explain to the change requester why
- If you decide to implement, define what work is needed to implement the change
- Update the project's various documents created during the planning step to reflect changes in human and non-human resources, costs, timelines
- Inform your team members of the change and the implications on them

If you are managing a project but do not own it, the steps discussed above work. Still, you might consider creating a committee made up of various stakeholders to review change requests and make recommendations to you. You might also consider then providing the recommendations to management for approval before implementing the requested changes.

Maintain Control Through Effective Communication to Minimize Conflict and Optimize Performance

Key to your project's success is keeping stakeholders informed throughout the project and creating an environment when they inform you and one another based on defined guidelines. We previously discussed the general communication process in step 3.8. We will now focus on the topic of project meetings.

About Meetings

Most meetings are not run effectively, waste time and other resources. Let's look at what you can do before, during, and after each meeting to optimize the meeting's benefits.

Before the meeting you should:
- Plan the meeting
- Define the goals of the meeting
- Define who will attend
- Determine if you can achieve the goal(s) without a meeting and if so, proceed accordingly
- Give notice to those requested to attend the meeting
- Explain the meeting's purpose to the attendees
- Prepare the agenda for the meeting
- Provide the agenda to those scheduled to attend

During the meeting you should:
- Start on time
- Keep it short
- Proceed according to the agenda
- Take notes or have notes taken

- Record action items (things that people need to do based on discussions made during meetings)
- Conclude on time

After each meeting, you should:
- Distribute minutes
- Monitor status of action items

Maintain Control Through Effective Leadership to Optimize Performance

Managing a project using the power you have given your financial resources is great. Managing a project using the power granted to you by those with the financial resources (your wife, your boss) is also great. On its own, however, such power is not sufficient to optimize performance since it often leads to jealousy which could lead to hate by others towards you and is likely to diminish their performance.

You should also provide your project's stakeholders with leadership! To lead is to motivate others to help you achieve a common goal.

Key Characteristics of a Leader

As a leader, you should ideally possess the following characteristics:
- Self-confidence
- Willingness to take risks
- Persistence

- Honesty
- Integrity
- High energy
- Enthusiasm

Why People Do What They Are Asked to Do?

You should understand why people might do what you ask them to do. These reasons include:

- Rewards
- Punishment
- Your position – your title in the organization
- What you stand for - your values
- Who you are - your personality
- Your expertise
- Any combination of the above

How Can you Establish Your Leadership?

To establish your leadership over others, you need to understand what you already have over them, as well as what else you need to have over them. You need to let them know things they do not yet know about you, and you need to get to know the things you do not yet know about them.

To motivate your stakeholders, you need to convey to them the value of achieving your common goals. You need to clarify to them the benefits of your project. Remember, the benefits may be clear to you, but they may not yet have your level of understanding of the project.

The benefits can be:
- For them as individuals – benefits such as making more money, learning and increasing experience, and more
- For the project
- For the team
- For the organization
- For society or a portion of it

Explain the likelihood of achieving the goal. Convey their accomplishments as they work to achieve the goal. Let them know how they are doing. Remind of the rewards for goals achieved and work well done.

Maintaining Control Through Effective Stakeholder Engagement

Your goal is to get each stakeholder and keep them at the desired engagement status to optimize their contributions to the project. It should also be your goal to minimize the damage they may cause the project should you lose their support.

Recall that each stakeholder's current and desired engagement status was discussed earlier in this step to achieve your stakeholder engagement goals.

Step 4.4 - Wrap Up the Project

Outline

> Keep Your Team Focused to the End
> Help Stakeholders Transition
> Conduct a Post-Project Evaluation

Introduction

Wrapping up, or closing a project, typically involves handling a multitude of small details, as well as some large issues.

Keep Your Team Focused to the End

You must constantly remind yourself of the project's objectives and stay focused on achieving them.

Prepare a checklist of everything to be done before the project is completed.

Help Stakeholders Transition

You should help team members transition to other projects. Let team members know in advance that you will help them with that. This can include any of the following:

- Let them know about the next project they will handle for you

- Find them another project to handle within the organization under the leadership of a different manager or project manager, and let them know about it
- Help them with a job search by providing a reference

You should also help the project's beneficiaries transition to use the project's deliverable(s). This can include the following:
- Training on the use of the deliverable(s)
- Videos about the deliverable(s)
- Instruction guide(s) / training materials

Conduct a Post-Project Evaluation

You should conduct a post-project evaluation – possibly a meeting with team members.

Step B – Adapt

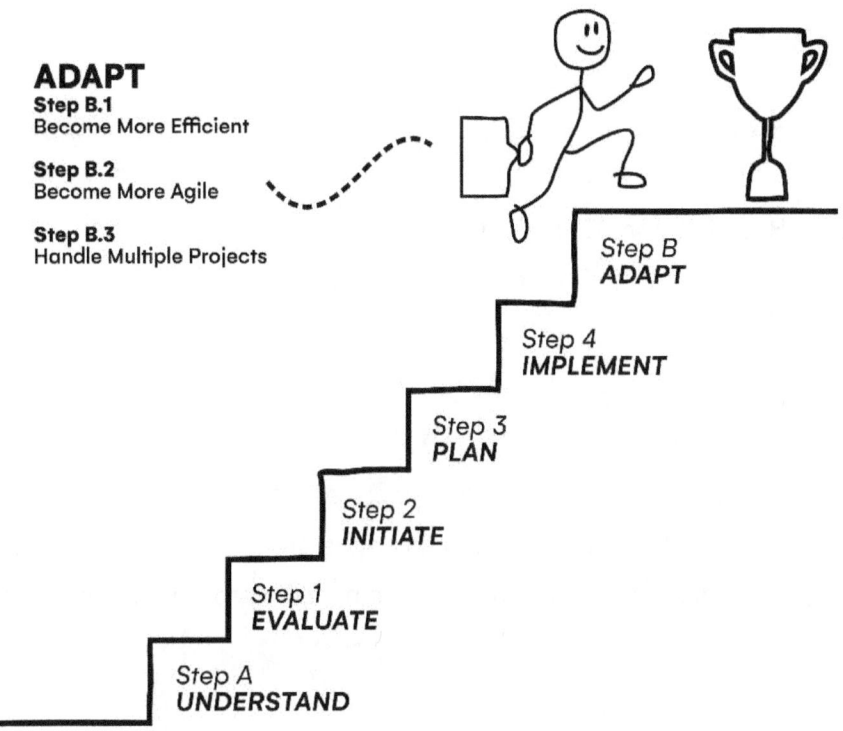

Step B - Overview

You will learn to become more efficient and agile in planning and implementing projects. You will also learn how to handle multiple projects.

Step B - Outline

Step B.1 - Become More Efficient and Agile with Future Projects
Step B.2 - Juggle Multiple Projects at the Same Time

Step B - Objectives

You should be able to explain how to be more efficient
You should be able to explain how to handle the project in a more agile manner
You should be able to explain how to handle multiple projects at the same time

Step B.1 - Become More Efficient and Agile with Future Projects

Outline

> Becoming Efficient with Future Projects
> Flexible (Agile) Approach to Project Management
> Frequent Update to Requirements
> Frequent Delivery of Subsets of the Final Deliverable
> Embracing Change Throughout the Project
> Embracing Increased Stakeholder Engagement Throughout the Project

Becoming Efficient with Future Projects

You likely did not learn to ride a bike in a day. You fell, again and again, and learned to balance yourself on your bike until one day, you stopped falling and were able to get from point A to point B much faster.

You should read the book more than once. Each time you do so, you will gain more clarity about the process. You should also use this book as a reference guide as you practice project management.

You might fall off the project management "bike" a few times before learning how to get from point A to point B quicker.

Flexible (Agile) Approach to Project Management

In the world of today and tomorrow, you need to be flexible (agile) with all that you do. This includes the way you manage your or other people's projects.

When it comes to project management, you should focus on the issues discussed in the next three sections.

Frequent Update to Requirements

Requirements are defined and modified frequently during all stages of the project. This is a change to the traditional approach to project management discussed earlier in the book. Frequent changes to requirements necessitate changes to many other planning documents we discuss earlier in the book.

Costs, timelines, risks, and other aspects of the project are modified on an ongoing basis throughout the project.

Frequent Delivery of Subsets of the Final Deliverable

Subsets of the final deliverable are created and provided. The final product is created and delivered incrementally for review and possible use if applicable. This is different than providing a final deliverable at the end of the project.

Embracing Change Throughout the Project

A culture of change is welcome. This means that stakeholders know that you welcome change and are willing to look at change requests during the project's duration. Changes once approved are incorporated throughout the project. This is different from traditional project management, where the project manager tries to minimize change once the project is approved.

Embracing Increased Stakeholder Engagement Throughout the Project

Key stakeholders are continuously involved throughout the project. This is different than in traditional project management, where many stakeholders are involved at major milestones only.

Step B.2 - Juggle Multiple Projects at the Same Time

Outline

> Coordinating Resources Across Projects
> Managing a Pipeline of Projects
> Delegating Project Management to Others

Introduction

Now that you know how to handle one project let's look at handling multiple projects.

Let's start by declaring that it is not practical to handle multiple projects at the same time. The key to success is to know how to organize, prioritize and switch between projects.

Coordinating Resources Across Projects

You have human resources working on one project, and you are starting the next project. You need to make a few decisions:
- Which resources from the first project do you need to work on the next project?
- When should you have them get started on the next project?
- Will this delay the first project? If so, are you ok with delaying the first project?

How you handle the next project and the next?

Managing a Pipeline of Projects

The process:
1. Review your list of projects/priorities
2. Reevaluate the priorities given your current situation
3. Select projects to initiate
4. Select projects to plan from those that were previously initiated
5. Select project(s) to implement from those that were previously planned

Project ID	Project Name	Priority	Status
			Evaluating
			Initiating
			Planning
			Implementing
			Closed

Delegating Project Management to Others

At a certain stage, you might decide that you do not want to or cannot handle the management of all the projects in your pipeline by yourself.

When do you delegate the management of projects? Which ones? To whom? There are questions you will need to answer.

You can still oversee the project managers, thus keeping yourself involved with some projects at a higher level.

If you have any ideas for improvement of this book, please email me at david@GeffenRealEstate.com or text me at 310-433-0694

If you enjoyed this book, please consider posting a review. Even if it's only a few sentences, it would be a huge help. Thank you.

Appendixes

Appendix A - Drawing of a Fence Section

The fence below (See Figure 14) shows the fence discussed in one of the two case studies throughout this book (A view from the front yard. The street is on the other side of the bushes).

Figure 14 - The Fence Discussed in this Book

The backside of this fence is shown next (See Figure 15)

Fence Section

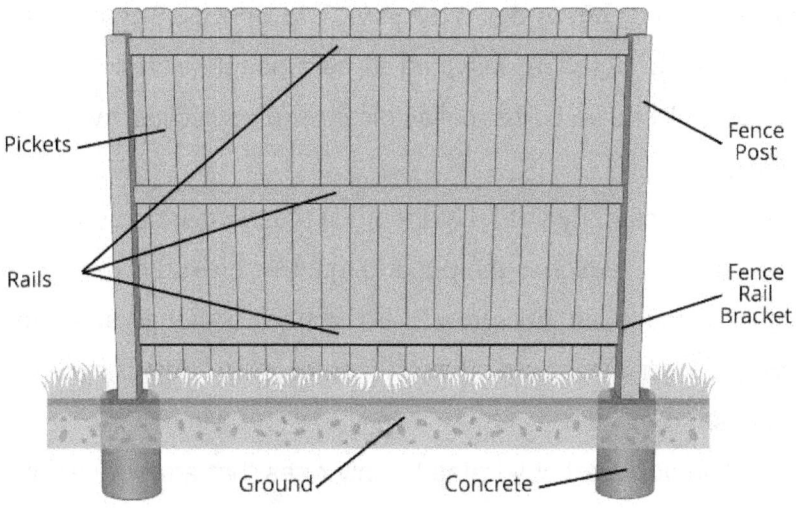

Figure 15 - Back of Fence (One Section)

Appendix B - SCD Diet Plan

According to WebMD.com (webmd.com/ibd-crohns-disease/crohns-disease/specific-carbohydrate-diet-overview) "The Specific Carbohydrate Diet is a restrictive, grain-free diet plan designed to help people with conditions such as Crohn's disease, ulcerative colitis, celiac disease, diverticulitis, cystic fibrosis, and chronic diarrhea.

The specific carbohydrate diet theory is that certain carbohydrates are not fully digested, so they remain in the gut and must be broken down by the bacteria there. This can cause an overgrowth of harmful bacteria, and the digestion process's waste products can set off a chain reaction, or "vicious cycle," of irritation in the intestines.

By limiting your carbohydrates to only ones that are very easily digested, the idea is that there will be no undigested carbohydrates left over to cause an overgrowth of bad bacteria and set off the chain reaction leading to irritation."

The SCD approach we chose comes from the following website: pecanbread.com/new/recipes.html

Appendix C – Project Management Related Deliverables Created When Managing a Project

The deliverables for each of the four core project management steps discussed in this book are presented in Figure 16 as well as in Figure 17, Figure 18, and Figure 19 below:

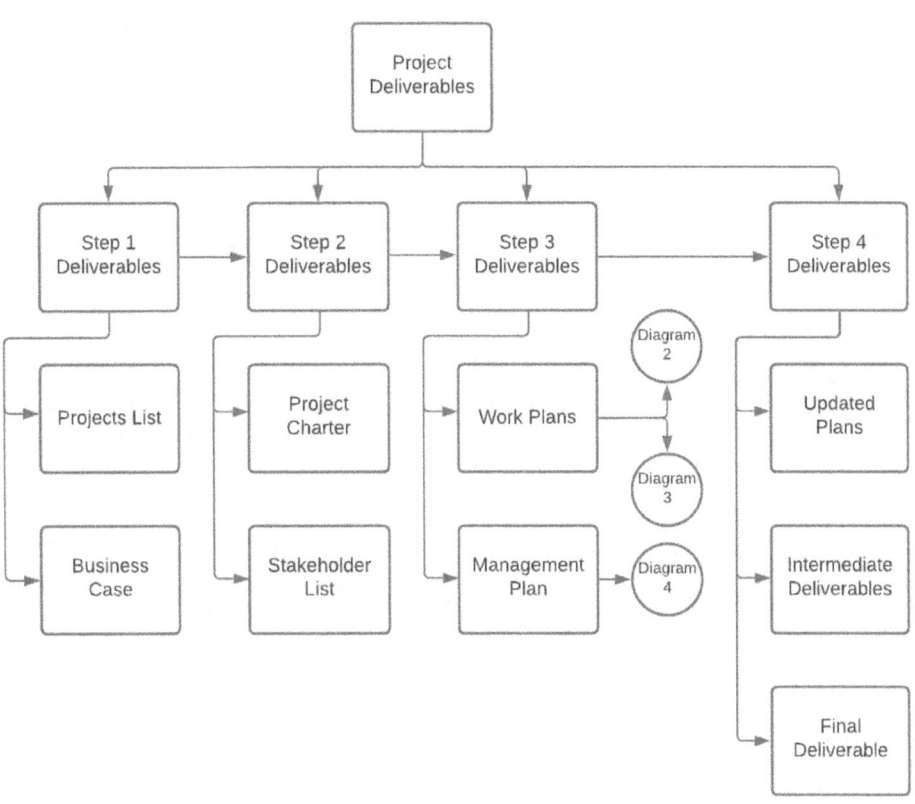

Figure 16 - Key Deliverables Created When Managing a Project (Diagram 1 of 4)

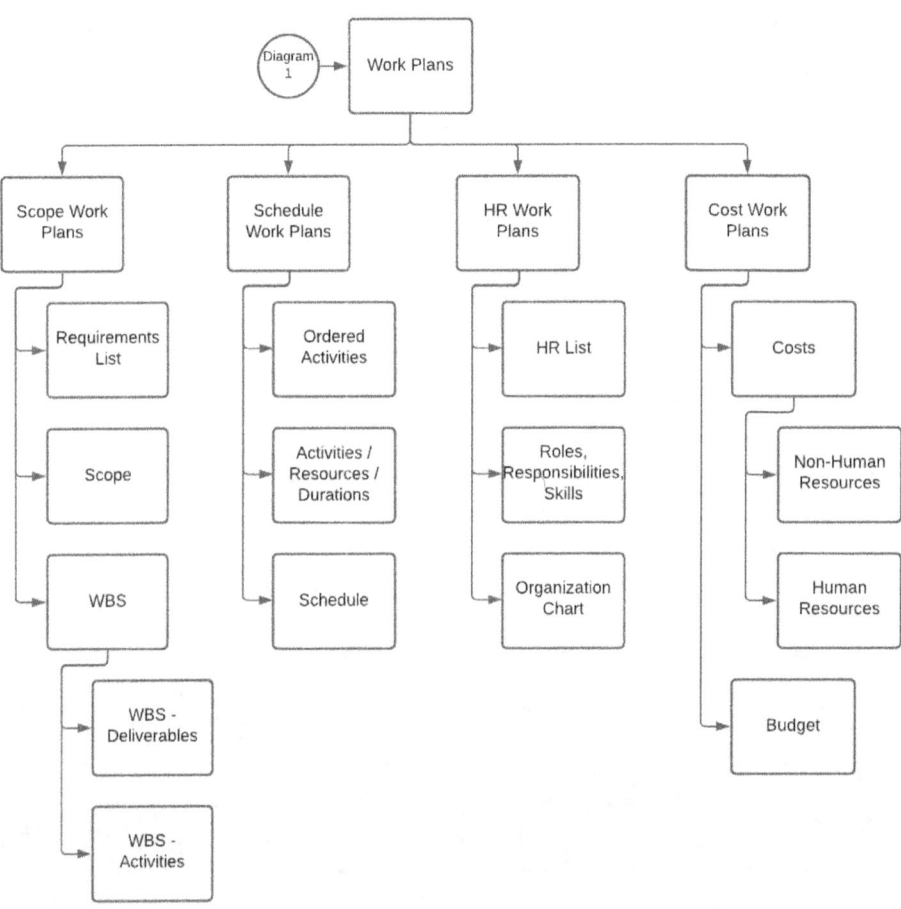

Figure 17 - Key Deliverables Created When Managing a Project (Diagram 2 of 4)

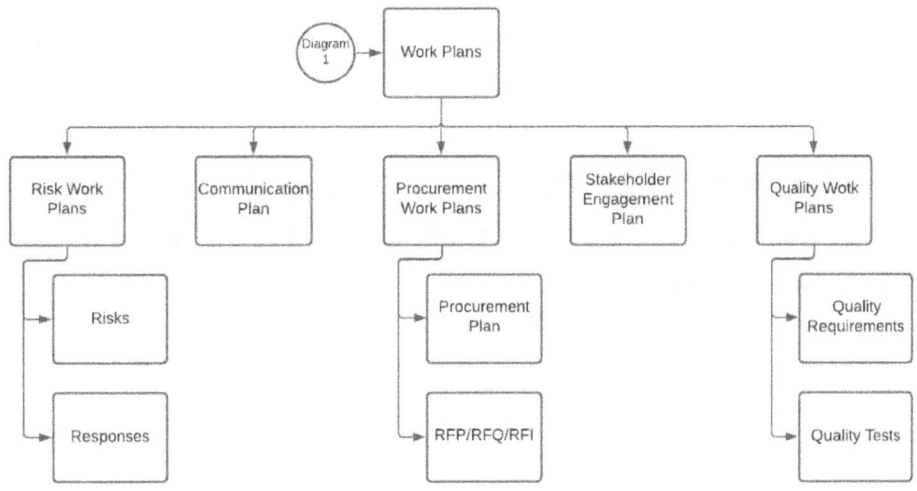

Figure 18 - Key Deliverables Created When Managing a Project (Diagram 3 of 4)

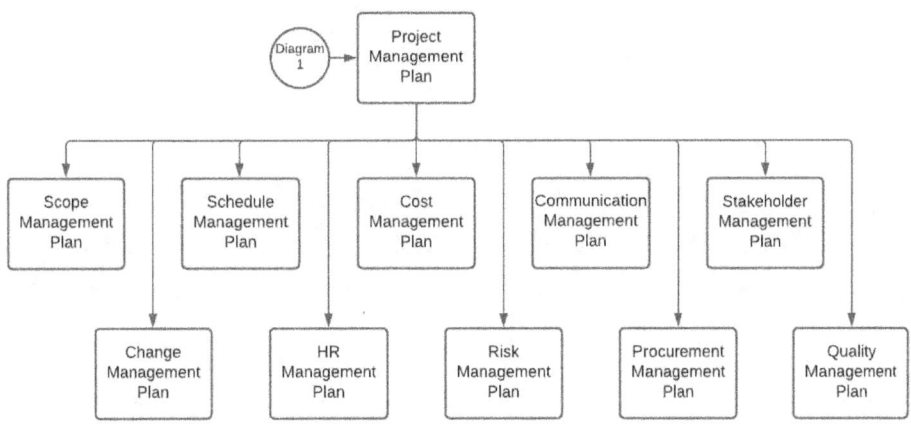

Figure 19 - Key Deliverables Created When Managing a Project (Diagram 4 of 4)

Appendix D – Project Management Related Activities Performed When Managing a Project

Key activities for each of the six steps discussed in this book is presented in Figure 20 below (Located on the next page to maximize the size of the figure on the page for your benefit):

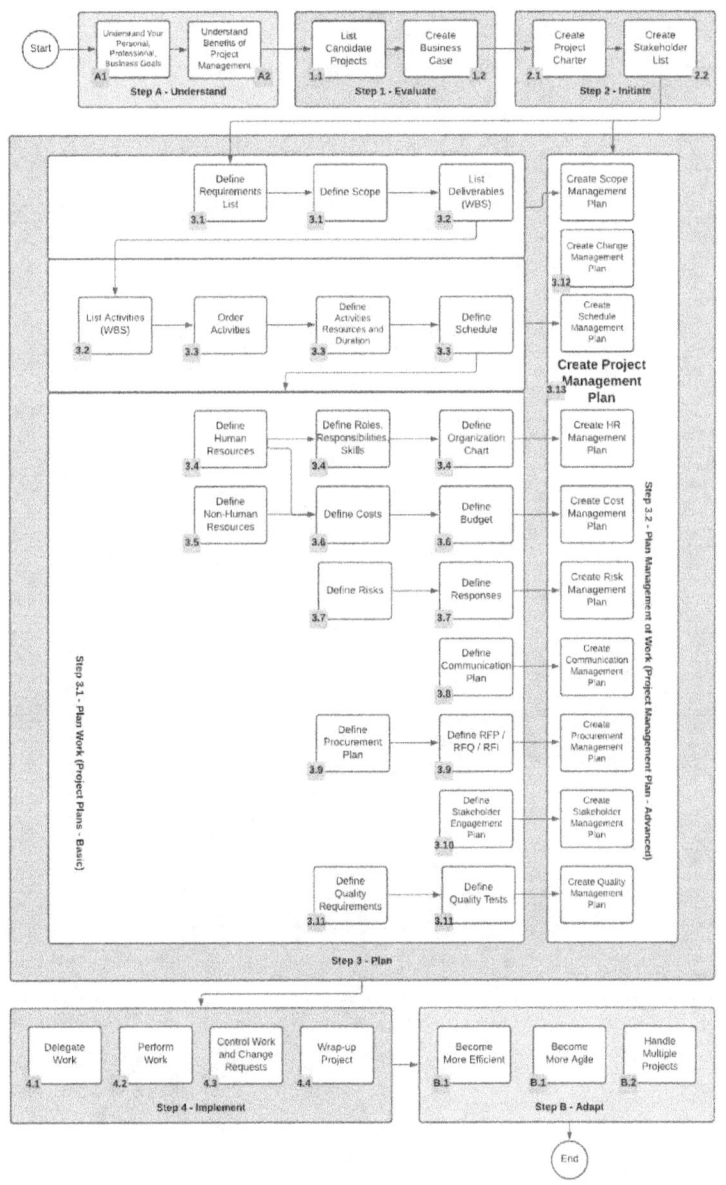

Figure 20 - Key activities for each of the 6 steps discussed in this book

www.ingramcontent.com/pod-product-compliance
Lightning Source LLC
Chambersburg PA
CBHW080732300426
44114CB00019B/2565